THE TOP OF THE ARC

THE TOP OF THE ARC

COCREATING A MORE INNOVATIVE, ADAPTIVE, AND EFFECTIVE LOCAL GOVERNMENT

SEAN R. STEGALL

RADIUS BOOK GROUP
NEW YORK

Radius Book Group
A Division of Diversion Publishing Corp.
www.RadiusBookGroup.com

Copyright © 2025 by Town of Cary, North Carolina

All rights reserved, including the right to reproduce this book or portions thereof in any form whatsoever. No part of this publication may be reproduced or transmitted in any form or by any means, electronic or mechanical, including photocopying, recording, or any other information storage and retrieval, without the written permission of the author.

For more information, email info@radiusbookgroup.com.

First Radius Book Group Edition: August 2025
Hardcover ISBN: 9798895150849
Ebook ISBN: 9798895150429

Manufactured in the United States of America

10 9 8 7 6 5 4 3 2 1

Cover design by Kristy Buchanan
Jacket design by Elizabeth Kingsbury
Interior design by Scribe Inc.

Radius Book Group and the Radius Book Group colophon are registered trademarks of Radius Book Group, a Division of Diversion Publishing Corp.

To all public servants, both elected and appointed, who tirelessly dedicate themselves to serving the public good. To my colleagues, both past and present, whose inspiration and wisdom I rely on daily. This book is dedicated to each of you, with gratitude and appreciation for your commitment to making a difference in the lives of those we serve.

And to my family, whose unwavering support and love keep me going every day.

CONTENTS

Preface ix

1. Shaping the Future 1
2. Local Government: Silos, Unity, and Opportunity 15
3. Communication, Good Governance, and 311 25
4. Cultural Change and Adapting to Cocreation 38
5. Getting the Culture Right: The OneCary Toolkit 48
6. Managing for Success 61
7. Consensus Building and Development 70
8. Changing the Horizons: Fenton and South Hills 81
9. How to Be a Good Town Manager 95
10. The Top of the Arc and the Importance of Reinvention 107

Acknowledgments 119
Notes 121

PREFACE

The subtitle for this book, "Cocreating a More Innovative, Adaptive, and Effective Local Government," wasn't my first choice, but it's the better choice. The original subtitle was "Creating the Local Government That Doesn't Exist," which is a phrase we use frequently in Cary to describe the purpose of our journey.

While working on this book, a friend remarked that "Creating the Local Government That Doesn't Exist" sounded like a "grassroots libertarian fantasy."

I laughed for two reasons. First, anyone who knows me knows I believe in good, effective, *proactive* governance. So let me get one thing out of the way right now: This is *not* a book advocating libertarian fantasies of tearing down or shrinking government. If anything, it's about local governments and the people they serve building the future together in more innovative, adaptive, and efficient ways.

The second reason I laughed was that I remembered the moment I blurted out the phrase, a completely off-the-cuff declaration. It was 2016, and I had just started my new job as town manager of Cary, North Carolina, a prosperous town just south of Research Triangle Park. I was at a meeting with members of the communications team, and I just tossed off the phrase. The funny thing was, once the words were out of my mouth, I wasn't even that crazy about them. I was riffing, trying to articulate my hope that in the future, Cary would create service models that hadn't been invented yet, programs and projects that would leave our citizens stunned—in a good way—by the results.

Preface

I wanted us to achieve things people simply never imagined a government could do.

As it turned out, the phrase resonated with the people in attendance. It was repeated, and pretty soon, people started asking me what it meant.

I'd bounce the question back at them: "What do you think it means?" I got a lot of different answers:

"It means we should aim high."

"I think it means you create a government so efficient and frictionless that people don't even realize it's there."

"It's a paradox, isn't it? How can you create something that doesn't exist?"

"I don't know, Sean! You're the one who said it!"

I welcomed all the interpretations, but those last two resonated. In North Carolina's council-manager form of government, the town manager functions as the chief executive officer of the municipal corporation. I'm the CEO who serves at the will of the Town Council and oversees all Cary operations and staff.[1] I am supposed to lead, not confuse, right?

As it happens, I find ambiguity, frustrating as it can be at times, is a great tool for getting people to think, to search for answers, and to listen to other points of view. That's why I asked the "What do you think it means?" question. I wasn't trying to be obtuse. I knew what I meant, but I was interested in what other people thought. And if they had no idea, I wanted them to wrestle with the phrase a bit. Working in local government isn't just about following rules, playing things safe, and always striving to maintain the status quo. It requires drive, insight, and vision. In the constantly morphing digital era, where computing power is estimated to double every two years and once-trendy products and platforms like the BlackBerry and the iTunes Store are suddenly eclipsed by the iPhone and subscription music apps, respectively, the only certainty is that change waits around most corners. One of government's most exciting and important roles involves discovering or uncovering new ideas, finding new solutions to improve the community, and collaborating with experts and innovators to learn about potential beneficial changes.

As the town manager, I make a habit of being very interested in other people's opinions. It's not just polite or politically savvy. It's smart. Because if every new idea and solution has to come from me, well, Cary is in trouble.

There is little doubt that some of the people who heard me utter the "doesn't exist" phrase thought it was absurd or that I had lost my mind. I'm surprised no one accused me of being downright delusional. As I have said more than once (and semipermanently on my LinkedIn page), "As Cary, North Carolina's CEO, I was hired to be a catalyst for change in a place where not only is nothing wrong but, by every measure, everything is nearly perfect."

This is not hyperbolic boosterism. Cary was, in metaphorical terms, at the top of the arc. It was at the highest point, the apex, of most metropolitan rankings. You can look it up. In the years before I arrived, Cary consistently showed up high on top-10 lists of ranking American cities: "Best Place to Live" (#2, *Wall Street Journal*), "Best Place to Retire" (#2, *Kiplinger*), and "Best Place to Raise a Family" (#1, *Forbes*), to name a few. The financial world admired Cary too. In 2001, all three major national bond rating agencies—Fitch, Moody's, and Standard & Poor's—awarded the town triple-A status, their highest ranking.

So why did I brazenly advocate messing with perfection?

The short answer is that the town told me to. It had looked back at the past and into the future, spending years developing Imagine Cary, a community-based initiative that began with 800 people attending a town meeting. Four hundred applications to join the steering committee, dozens of polls and interviews, and hundreds of meetings later, it ended in the adoption of a policy guide for the future: the Imagine Cary Community Plan.

Preface

A slightly longer answer involves evoking the actual title of this book, *The Top of the Arc*, and the daunting reality of a curving trajectory, which is what an arc is: a path that rises and falls. Staying at the top of an arc—which is to say, *not falling*—is a very difficult thing to sustain for any length of time in business, in government, in sports. Just ask a surfer. Every wave they ride rises, crests, and then runs out of momentum.

To me, Cary's ability to stay at the top of the arc—providing excellent services and quality of life for our citizens—is tied to creating the local government that doesn't exist. Yes, the Cary Community Plan codified a development strategy. But enacting that strategy required collaborating on a new, foundational culture. One that, to use a quote popularized by Council Member Jennifer Bryson Robinson, would "wait for great" instead of just settling for "good." One that would strive to deliver positive experiences and outcomes for all, building and developing projects that aimed high, hit the targets, and in doing so, lifted the town up.

For the last eight years, I have focused on leading Cary into the future, turning our plans into realities. In that time, we have created a new, centralized 311 communications system for the town to document and share information across the organization. We built a world-class public park in the center of Downtown Cary that was 3 times the size and 10 times the budget of the original plan. We helped launch the first vertical—as in buildings higher than three stories—mixed-use development in town history, with apartment buildings, streets lined with top-tier retail outlets, a million square feet of office space, a skating rink, and a multiplex.

And that's just some of what we've done—or should I say, created? Because none of it existed previously in Cary.

I wrote this book with three goals in mind: (1) to tell the story of Cary, documenting a pivotal moment after 45 years of unprecedented growth, and share the lessons learned to help other towns across America create a local government that doesn't exist; (2) to offer lessons and best practices for local government, including the OneCary Toolkit; and (3) to advocate for people-first, adaptive leadership at the local level to inspire and deliver positive outcomes to, in effect, rise to the top of the arc and stay there.

It took a while for these three goals to coalesce.

The first time someone suggested I write a book about Cary and creating a local government that doesn't exist, I rejected the idea immediately. What would I know about writing a book? Several other people brought up the idea, and I thought, "Hmm, maybe they are serious." A few months later, Town Council Member Lori Bush, who I knew read a lot about business and leadership, told me, "Sean, you should write a book." Lori, of course, is one of my bosses. Who was I to argue with her? I thought about it some more, and I decided sharing Cary's journey and my experiences as a town manager might be helpful and empowering for the town. We deserved to see what we've done put down in black and white. Also, I thought our efforts here might be instructive for other local governments.

Embracing the idea, I realized I had to practice what I preached about getting out of comfort zones and trying new things. As leadership experts might put it, I needed to model the behavior I wanted to encourage.

But I had one nonnegotiable demand. I wanted to work with someone who had collaborated on books about politics, current events, and social movements. As I hope the stories in this book demonstrate, I believe Cary, and all organizations, can benefit from working with experts. I didn't plan Downtown Cary Park or any other town initiative by myself. And I sure wasn't going to write a book alone either.

My main reason for hiring a collaborator was that I wanted a sounding board to listen to the story I wanted to share, bear witness, and help shape it for a wider audience. I knew that as the primary author, I would be telling Cary's story—or my version of that story. But I also wanted the insights and opinions of colleagues and experts who have worked with Cary and with me—other people who would remember things differently or bring new perspectives.

Preface

And I knew that if I interviewed those people about Cary, they might not tell me exactly what they thought. Or if they said flattering things, I'd look like a self-serving egotist for including them in the book. That was definitely not my goal!

So the quotes in this book from people not named Sean were obtained and selected by a journalist and best-selling ghostwriter who conducted hours of interviews to learn about Cary. My collaborator has discussed me behind my back, with my blessing. He asked people for criticism on or off the record. He didn't get as much as either of us hoped. Apparently, I'm not very controversial in Cary. The lack of controversy may prove bad for book sales, but it gives me confidence about my performance as town manager. And confidence is important. It is an underappreciated resource. Believing in yourself, your town, your vision is a vital first step toward creating a new, better local government.

I realize that not all towns in America have the same resources in terms of wealth, budget, revenue, and infrastructure. The town of Camden, New Jersey, is going to have different priorities and challenges than the affluent suburb of Greenwich, Connecticut. That said, if Cary's transformation is not necessarily duplicative, there are many lessons that are instructive—about people, culture, process, how to harness data and adaptive strategies—for town governments of all shapes and sizes.

At the top of the arc and at the core of local government are people. They are our greatest resource. If there is one thing I hope to show in this book, it's that leaders can optimize organizations and achieve their visions by empowering people to succeed. This is not a wholly original concept. I was inspired by Ronald Heifetz and Marty Linsky's book *Leadership on the Line*, which advises that adaptability in an uncertain, ever-changing world is the key to successful transformations. Similarly, in 1993, David Osborne, an advisor to Al Gore, wrote a book called *Reinventing Government* that called for civil service to borrow private sector principles. He was advocating adaptive leadership too, just using business paradigms, such as seeking to understand customers (a.k.a.

Preface

citizens), not confusing efficiency with effectiveness, and weighing concepts like the return on investment.

Speaking of return on investment, I have been inspired by the people of Cary, the Cary Town Council, and my colleagues in our local government who strive to invent a better future. Instilling confidence and support isn't a one-way street. It is reciprocal. When the Council supports my vision, it is truly empowering. I believe in sharing that energy, in encouraging people to aim high and dream big—perhaps bigger than they could ever imagine. And when that transformation becomes reality, well, I can't help myself.

I want to do something even bigger.

I hope this book encourages readers to think the same way.

CHAPTER 1
SHAPING THE FUTURE

That was kind of a phenomenon of Cary. When you study other towns that had similar fast growth, where I think a lot of them failed is that they never got their new people involved. And either because of our boards and commissions or the way we were organized, we did that. We seemed to have a way to draw out these new people, and a lot of them had great talent.

—Jack Smith, nine-term Cary Town Council member

The American town you live in has a singular history. It was created and settled under a unique set of circumstances by a specific set of individuals. It exists in a unique geographical space surrounded by other unique geographical spaces. It is populated by people with different backgrounds. It is part of 1 of 50 states or 14 territories, each with separate laws, taxes, and infrastructures.

Our towns share many things in common, but there are only two universal traits: all towns are unique, and all towns change. Even the most rural, ignored, no-new-development-in-decades town mutates. If nothing else, it gets older.

Not even a town council—or a town manager—can stop time.

I mention this because, for the rest of this book, 98 percent of the action is going to be rooted in Cary, North Carolina, and a good deal of

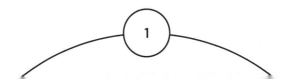

the subject matter will revolve around change or, to use my preferred term, evolution. In my view, *evolution*—as opposed to the favorite buzzword of every political and business expert, *transformation*—implies a state of constant positive change, not simply "transforming" from one state to another. While the specifics are going to be about Cary's evolution, I want readers to know that many aspects of what occurred—how we changed the culture, how we decentralized leadership, how we aimed higher with each project, how we embraced new advisors and explored what other towns were doing—are practices any town can adopt or adapt as needed.

WHY IMAGINE THE FUTURE?

As I said in the preface, Cary told me it wanted to change. Years before I'd even set foot in town limits, an initiative called the Imagine Cary Community Plan was underway.

It was an impressive undertaking. By definition, planning for the future is not something humans—and the organizations they run—are particularly good at. When do people start dieting or quit smoking? Quite often, *after* they have a heart attack. When does a busy intersection get new traffic lights? *After* a dozen fender benders.

The launch of Imagine Cary was, whether the Council knew it or not, a declaration of an independent future: a town's existential dream to stay ahead of the curve and control its destiny.

Here's how the news release for the town-wide 2013 invitation to the Summit on the Future described the project:

> The Summit on the Future is a part of Imagine Cary, the name given by the citizen steering committee to the town's unprecedented approach to updating the community's comprehensive plan. Working with consultant team Clarion Associates, Cary will gain feedback from citizens, businesses and others with a connection to the town on a wide range of topics and

Shaping the Future

issues related to the town's future, such as land use, community development, transportation, housing, environment, economic development, and related topics. At the end of two years, these diverse planning efforts will be crafted into a single overarching community vision to be known as the Cary Community Plan, which will help guide the town for the next 20–30 years.[1]

This summit was three years in the making. In late 2010, the Town of Cary realized it faced several significant planning issues. The following year, it directed the staff to update the previous 1995 Land Use Plan completely. Then the town did something astounding. It formulated a two-step process to determine how best to involve the ultimate stakeholders—town residents—to report the scope of the project. This included how to approach the project and an outline of the ultimate deliverable: the content and format for the new, comprehensive plan. That was stage one.

Stage two, then, was to literally Imagine Cary; the only way to succeed was to engage the stakeholders.

Nearly 800 people registered on the imaginecary.org website to attend the meeting. Participants received remote devices to log their feedback on specific issues, such as how the town should attract new business or deal with an aging population. They also heard a talk by Chris Leinberger, a noted urban strategist, Brookings Institute senior fellow, and professor at George Washington University's Center for Real Estate and Urban Analysis. Leinberger shared his thoughts on "new urbanism," a movement that advocates, among other things, "walkable" urban development to create towns where most daily needs can be met without using a car. A proponent of smart growth, Leinberger believed focusing on walkable urbanism would promote a town's sustained economic development and, with it, social equity, public health, and environmental resilience.

For many in attendance, the meeting was profoundly affecting. It pointed to new paradigms, new visions, and new opportunities. But it was also something of a shock. Cary's housing stock of single-family homes—one of its calling cards—was fabulous. But those houses defined the area; the town was sprawling, with a low center of gravity and a huge dependence on cars. The tallest structures were schools and church steeples. Envisioning an urban future that focused on growing up, not out, took exactly what the initiative adopted as its name: imagination.

That shock caused some initial reverberations. The *Cary News*, a local paper, ran a front-page story titled "Cary Fielding Backlash after Summit," reporting that some attendees took issue with Leinberger's "new urbanist" focus and viewed it as overly or preemptively influencing the planning initiative. Council Member Ed Yerha described the featured speaker as "offensive." Council Member Jack Smith, however, denied any secret agenda, telling the paper, "The planning process does not have any set objectives."

Despite that apparent hiccup (remember, I wasn't here at the time), the initiative did not lose steam. It kept rolling with meetings, drafts, and more meetings. Eventually, committee members crafted a very long-term plan, delivering a blueprint with a modified name, the Cary 2040 Community Plan, which we now refer to as the Imagine Cary Community Plan.

As a guy with a master's in public administration who helped manage two midsized cities in the Northeast and Midwest, I can tell you that what Cary did was exceedingly rare. Detailed municipal blueprints that attempt to lay out a town's vision, values, challenges, and solutions *decades into the future* don't happen in small-town America or in major cities. Even in China, where 5- and 10-year plans are usually *national* initiatives, a 25-year municipal plan is pretty much unheard of.

What fueled Imagine Cary or the initial "We need a new plan" idea back in 2010?

Simply put, Cary was exploding, both in size and in population.

In 1975, 14,700 people lived in the 7.94 square miles (5,080 acres) that made up the town's entire footprint. By 2010, a mere 35 years later, there were 135,234 people in Cary, according to the US Census, and the town had expanded to 55.4 square miles.[2] Twelve years later, the population was 180,388. (And now, as I write, we are over 190,000.)

These remarkable numbers are the result of an average 6.5 percent annual growth rate over those 35 years. Cary had become a coveted community. Part of this was due to the perfect storm of timing and location. Cary fell in the footprint of North Carolina's Research Triangle region—just west of our state capital, Raleigh; south of Research Triangle Park; and within easy driving distance of Chapel Hill, Durham, Raleigh-Durham International Airport, and a slew of prestigious universities. The business-friendly environment, bolstered by low taxes and other incentives, attracted hundreds of businesses. Research Triangle Park reportedly averaged six new companies and 1,800 new employees annually.[3] As companies such as GlaxoSmithKline, Cisco, Lenovo, and Oracle set up operations there, Cary was a logical community for new arrivals. Cary itself also served as the headquarters of several digital companies, including SAS Institute, the software giant launched in 1976; Epic Games, the video gaming behemoth booted up in 1991; and DataFlux, the internet and software services firm started in 1997.

Cary's influx of commerce and development was and is vital to the community. And no doubt, some will view money as a primary catalyst for Imagine Cary. Indeed, the second sentence of the final document's vision statement says, "The interests of residents and businesses will be at the forefront of policies and public investment that foster sustained prosperity." But I believe something else drove the town as it assembled 12 essential values—which included concerns about "Managing Future Land Use," "Encouraging Redevelopment and Infill Efforts," "Protecting Nature," and "Providing Comprehensive and Top Quality Facilities and Infrastructure"—and codified them in a vision statement that served as a springboard to issue this 25-year development plan.

I'm very people-focused. I believe in them. And I credit Imagine Cary purely to its citizens and its Town Council. Census data tells us that about 90 percent of the people who reside in Cary come from somewhere else. Only 10 percent of the populace are native Caryites. That low percentage suggests there was no critical mass to ensure an entrenched power structure. Sure, the Methodist and Baptist churches, the closest thing to communal glue in the town, carried some clout. But there was no political machine, no union-driven kingmakers, no single company employer that tried to dominate the Town Council.

Just because 90 percent of Cary residents are newcomers doesn't mean Cary was or is a transient community. Many new arrivals stay. And many of these residents, who the 2010 census tells us had a median household income of $120,817 ($30,000 more than the national average), had come of age in an era of innovation. The companies they worked for focused on driving change. And to a certain extent, they embraced change just by moving to Cary. This shared experience of coming from somewhere else, of wanting to be invested in their community, and, perhaps, of feeling empowered at their places of work allowed this visionary document to flourish. People had ideas about what they wanted their community to be. In effect, they came together to forge a plan that foreshadowed my own vision.

They started down the path of creating something that didn't exist. They just didn't phrase it that way.

WATER EQUALS DESTINY

There was one other event in Cary's history that put the town in a position to imagine writing its future in such a commonsense (and yet somehow audacious) manner.

In the late 1980s, the town decided that to control its own growth, it needed to control its own water supply. Jack Smith, a Cary Town Council member who has held the office continuously since 1989, told me he considers it the most important local government action to occur during his nine terms—that's 36 years—of service.

He said, "Mayor Koka Booth, the mayor at the time I joined the Council, saw that for us to cope with the growth, we needed to be responsible for our infrastructure, which basically meant water. All of us in the area, we were beholden to Raleigh."

In other words, any development initiative in Cary that involved, say, new water lines—which was pretty much every development ever—would require approval from Raleigh's Public Utilities Department, now also known as Raleigh Water.

"There was a lot of bureaucracy about being able to break away and have your own independent water system," Smith recalled, estimating it took 10 years for Cary to gain control of an autonomous water system. "*Fighting* is probably too strong a word, but we did a lot of work with the state government to get the approval to break away from Raleigh and then had to work with all the environmental organizations."

The town also drafted support from our neighbor, Apex, cutting them in on part ownership of what is now the Cary/Apex Water Treatment Facility, which now moves up to 56 million gallons per day.

"That experience developed the foundation for critical thinking and the complex thinking in Cary," Smith said. "The next thing that came along was wastewater, and we used the lessons learned from acquiring water to get that done. So now we have water and wastewater, and we have control of our destiny. Most cities don't have that, and we are blessed with that to this day.

"We have a lot that we can be thankful for in planning and urban planning and all the other stuff. But controlling our access to water is the foundation that gave us the ability to be successful."

Cary's population has nearly tripled since the town began its quest for water independence. More than 130,000 people have moved in since that journey started, bringing our population to over 190,000 people. If Raleigh still had the power to approve all the water and wastewater lines in town, that number would very likely be much lower, and the Cary story would be much different. The pace of development and the empowering sense of autonomy would not be as strong as they are.

There's no way to know for certain, but I wonder if the town would have embarked at all on Imagine Cary without having its own water system. When another city controls your infrastructure, you are at their mercy.

Thankfully, that was no longer the case.

ADDING ACRES

There's one other aspect of Cary's growth worth mentioning: the town's footprint. How did Cary balloon from 7.9 square miles in 1975 to 42.9 square miles in 2000 to 62.1 square miles in 2024? Basically, the town annexed surrounding land in Wake County that was not affiliated with any other municipality.

"North Carolina used to allow cities to initiate an annexation process," said Scot Berry, Cary's chief development officer, when asked to explain the growth spurt. "As long as you could provide the services, you were able to expand the footprint of your city. So for a long period of time, from the '90s through the early 2000s, we were doing a lot of annexation cases. Some of these cases were contentious, involving people who didn't necessarily want to become part of Cary. These people were reaping the benefits of living close to Cary. They were using Cary streets, using Cary parks. If there was a fire in a nearby house, our Cary Fire Department would respond to it. So it makes sense, from a community planning perspective, to incorporate these communities into Cary, since the town was already providing some key services."

As Cary expanded, the uneven growth and new borders of the town created geographical doughnut holes—areas that were sometimes completely surrounded by Cary but weren't part of the town. This was problematic and inefficient. "The town was providing services all the way around, but not in the middle," Berry said. "If you think about picking up trash, the efficient thing is to pick up all the houses, right? And not have to go, 'All right, do this one, but not this one next door.' You have to provide water, sewer, fire, police. Those were key things you had to provide to a citizen in order to annex them. So having our water plant and building our water and sewer lines is sort of what puts our stake in the ground."

Those pillars of infrastructure are extremely important. Berry stated, "When I started in Cary in 2002, we had 94,000 people. So over my career, we've added 100,000 people to the population. If you think about the difference between a 90,000-person community and a 200,000-person community, that's just a vast challenge in the types of services people anticipate and that you, as a town, must be able to provide."

NEW STAKEHOLDERS, NEW VISIONS, BETTER OUTCOMES

I want to point out that Cary is not the only town with a sizable population influx.

In fact, many communities in America have high percentages of newcomers. America is a country on the move. In 2022, 2.5 percent of the US population relocated to a different state, the largest percentage in the last 10 years.[4] It's a safe bet that this increase was propelled by a variety of issues, from postpandemic restlessness to new work opportunities, and from housing affordability to the quest for lower taxes—which may be why Florida and Texas experienced the biggest newcomer increases. Activating the community is a best practice for towns that are growing younger and more populous. Getting residents engaged and feeling heard empowers the town and its citizens. The local government should desire participation. This is an important feedback loop. Otherwise, how does a town know who it is serving and what is desired?

Imagine Cary was a feedback loop initiated by the local government. It gathered intelligence, it formulated policy, it provided vision. It was ready to be activated.

TURNING PLANS INTO REALITY

In 2016, I was invited to interview for the job of Cary town manager.

For the second time.

I was the town manager of Elgin, Illinois, the sixth-largest municipality in the state, with a population of 116,000. And I'd applied for the Cary job months earlier. But my primary competition in that initial round managed a ritzy town near Chicago. I knew the odds were against me. If this was a beauty contest, the other candidate's town was much prettier and better known than Elgin. He got the initial offer, but in the end, he didn't get the job.

I had impressed some of the Caryites I'd met in the first round, and I was invited to interview again, which was gratifying. When I returned for a new round of interviews with the Council, the first question was, "What's your management style?"

"I'm going to have fun," I said with a smile. "If you hire me as town manager, we are going to have so much fun. Count on it."

I'm pretty sure that was not the answer they expected. But I wanted to exude confidence. And frankly, I was confident. I knew I had a good track record of being a successful second choice—ask my wife, Michele; I was her second choice too, and it worked out pretty well.

Still, they were serious and cautious and asked for additional written responses to the following questions: "What do you think of Imagine Cary?" "What are the obstacles to implementing the initiative?" and "How would you manage development initiatives and the expectations around those initiatives?" As I answered them, I had an epiphany about Imagine Cary. The questions had a nervousness to them, and I realized why.

Remember my example of the guy who decides to diet only after surviving a heart attack? Even though it's a life-and-death matter, some people struggle to do what they need to do. They stumble on their diets. It's human nature.

Similarly, based on my understanding of government, I knew that even though many people say they need or want to change, they don't know how to do it. They don't have the discipline, the skill set, or the will. And at the end of the day, some of them, understandably, don't want to. It's easier just doing things the old way. The Imagine Cary initiative wasn't a diet. It was, long term, a radical makeover, an ambitious 25-year vision that was essential to Cary's continued prosperous evolution. I looked at those questions and recalled my conversations with the

Council. I had the sense that they needed someone to lead—a personal trainer, to extend the metaphor—who could reshape the local government and thereby help reshape the town. Without that person, they worried their six-years-in-the-making blueprint for the future would be little more than a 276-page exercise manual that nobody ever read.

THE REST IS MAKING HISTORY

To state the obvious, I got the town manager job. Months later, on January 24, 2017, the Town Council voted to adopt Imagine Cary's crystallized work: *The Cary 2040 Community Plan: A Comprehensive Plan for the Town of Cary*. It is a remarkable document. (Full disclosure: Although I am one of dozens acknowledged in the report, it was primarily written before I joined the team.)

The opening chapter, "Foundations," lays out an overview of Cary's past and present and the challenges posed by the future. For me, a section entitled "Future Fiscal Challenges" distills perhaps the critical driver behind the entire plan. Noting Cary's 40 years of growth, the report states,

> The Town's revenues increased along with property valuations, covering the expenses of delivering additional services and maintaining existing infrastructure. An estimated 80% of that revenue growth, on average, has been generated by the addition of [a] new tax base to the Town. In fact, the Town has seen a direct correlation between population growth and tax revenue growth. As Cary runs out of land for development and enters a new phase of slower growth in the next 10 to 20 years, the Town could experience a declining rate of revenue growth. Meanwhile, the cost of providing services and maintaining infrastructure like parks and recreation and water and sewer service is expected to rise and the annual increase in costs could eventually surpass the increase in revenues at current tax

rates. Added to the challenge is demand for increasing services and new community amenities, and an aging infrastructure that will require future maintenance investments. Cary's challenge will be to identify fiscally sustainable revenue generation models supported by the community that can continue to provide high quality services and facilities to existing and future residents.[5]

Of the nine remaining chapters in the document, eight are dedicated to shaping the future of specific critical aspects of Cary. "Live," for example, is focused on fostering strong neighborhoods given the challenges of an aging population, increased ethnic and racial diversity, and the demands for new housing stock. "Work," subtitled "Assuring Continued Prosperity," declares the town will "support expansion and business recruitment efforts by providing 21st-century workplaces and community amenities that meet the needs of future businesses and workers." Other chapters focus on the future of shopping; public engagement initiatives for parks, sports, and other cultural resources; how different areas will be developed; transportation needs; and serving other community needs. Each chapter has multiple sections, including "Challenges and Opportunities" and a concluding "How We Will Achieve Our Vision."

The plan was posted online. The road map for an evolving Cary was available to all. Now we had to start navigating.

NAYSAYERS AND YAYSAYERS

Our journey, however, wasn't without bumps and blocks in the road.

Just because our elected Town Council had passed Imagine Cary, which was based on extensive input from members of the Cary community and ignited by the real-world events of shifting populations and demographics and an economic boom, didn't mean everyone was on board.

Shaping the Future

There was a small, vocal group who seemed to want to freeze time. To deny the evolution that our elected leaders supported.

It was shocking to me that these naysayers seemed to believe that Cary could simply stay the same and maintain the status quo. Look at any city or town in America. Very few places look like they did in 1955. Or even 1975. And if they do, it's usually because the community is enormously wealthy and has ironclad policies to prevent development or because it's very poor and is slowly eroding.

On the internet, articles about Imagine Cary appeared that treated urbanization as a sinister conspiracy, one designed purely to foster public-private development and increase population density—two things that critics seemed to tie to quality-of-life concerns.

A website sprung up posting alarmist and misguided articles asserting Cary's population would "explode." One article linked to a clip of Cary's planning and zoning chairman Mark Evangelista saying, "We're going to get another 100,000 people in this town in about the next 10 to 15 years, and we've got to put them somewhere. And as you heard, there's only 18 percent of our town left to put stuff in." The site then conflated Mark's words into a disturbing narrative: "This nearly doubles Cary's population, into a small fraction of our space. It will be an influx equivalent to two thirds of our current population, stacked up in one sixth of the space we now share.

"This compares to the density of Washington, DC, and double the population density of Detroit."

A later calculation states, "Cary now has about 1.7 households per acre of land. These high density zones will house 5.8 households per acre."[6]

The authors wanted it to sound like the sky was falling. It wasn't. Nobody ever said *all newcomers were going to be exclusively shoehorned into Cary's undeveloped land.* These projections—misguided scare tactics—read as if our town was planning to erect some kind of urban ghetto. It was as if the writer had never heard of *redevelopment*—the concept of redefining and repurposing existing land. Did the writer think our 1980s strip malls were sacrosanct—the Cary equivalent

The Top of the Arc

of the Taj Mahal or the Empire State Building—and would never be repurposed?

These misinformation efforts would have been laughable if I didn't suspect the people behind the website were inspired by a rabid fear of "urbanization" and "undesirable outsiders" moving into town.

Instead of embracing Cary's Council members who voted to enact its citizens' ambitious and aspirational recommendations to improve the town and enhance our collective quality of life, these critics attempted to unseat them. The website accused the Mayor and Town Council of representing special interests. It accused the Council of sticking Cary's citizens with the bill for any development, but the writers never seemed to consider what citizens might get in return, such as new infrastructure, entertainment venues, shopping venues, and housing stock.

In the end, the creators of the site recommended voting out Council members who supported Imagine Cary and named names—while refusing to sign their own.

I'm pleased to say the bad faith arguments, the baseless accusations of selling out the town to private interests, and the fearmongering about an urban invasion gained no traction. Good governance keeps its eyes on the prize by following well-honed processes that evaluate and safeguard projects. I will talk in more detail about those processes in future chapters. But the bottom line is that Imagine Cary was created in an open, forthright manner by people who aimed to serve the town, not tear it down.

In the end, Cary got to work and stayed busy.

So busy that, a few years later, I bumped into a former Town Council member who said, "I'm only half joking, but if I knew you were actually going to implement Imagine Cary, I never would have voted for it."

CHAPTER 2
LOCAL GOVERNMENT

SILOS, UNITY, AND OPPORTUNITY

It was a culture shift. But obviously, the bulk of the town really embraced it. They were like, "This is really cool. What? I get to spend time learning about leadership and about how I can do my job better? I get to try something different, in an entirely different department? Really?" That was not even an opportunity previously. That was never even thought of.

—Lori Bush, four-term Cary Town Council member

When I arrived in Cary, I felt incredibly lucky. Not just about my present situation and the blue-sky future detailed by Imagine Cary—which, in many ways, felt like winning the lottery—but about my past. My previous jobs and a life-changing educational encounter had inspired me to believe that a new type of local government wasn't just possible but necessary.

Prior to Cary, I had been the assistant town manager in St. Charles, Illinois, a bustling semimetropolis of 33,000 people located 40 miles west of Chicago, and Batavia, New York, a town of 16,000 at the midpoint between Buffalo and Rochester. From there, I went to Elgin,

Illinois, where I spent nearly nine years as assistant city manager before getting the top job in 2009.

In Elgin, my initial responsibilities were split between serving as the budget director and doing things nobody else wanted to do. I became the public information officer. I had no business doing either of these things. I had no fiduciary or accounting background and very little formal training with communications, which lies at the core of sharing information with the public.

I quickly realized that both of these tasks were of premium importance to the members of the city council. They cared about budgets because, newsflash, money changes everything—it funds schools, roads, policing, sanitation, and anything else a city does. Naturally, they cared about messaging because that influences voters and voters can change city councils. As it happened, my first boss in Elgin wasn't very politically savvy. She hated dealing with council members, which was ironic. Like it or not, being a city or town manager is never a purely supervisory position—it is extremely political. The job entails influencing the actions and policies of the local government; that's what politics is. And the council members are the people who ultimately approve actions and policies. They are also every town manager's boss. So establishing a smooth working relationship with the council is an essential part of the job. It is also part and parcel of a functioning representative democracy.

I began working closely with many council members. They would come to me with questions. They would come to me with requests. I discovered something important: The best form of diplomacy starts with being available. With answering the phone. With arranging a meeting. Those interactions may have started as one-way diatribes on the part of a council member, but a request or demand or rant might lead to a clarifying question, which might lead to alternative options. Eventually, a dialogue, a conversation, might break out.

And from where I was sitting, every exchange was a good exchange.

My boss in Elgin didn't see it that way, and she wasn't alone. A close friend of mine has worked in senior positions for five different town managers. In her experience, managers typically saw themselves as being in charge and erecting an invisible wall to keep the council a very long arm's length away. As she put it, "It was as if the manager said, 'Council, you don't get to come into my world. I will bring you things that I think you need to know about at least once a year so you can vote on a budget. But even when I bring it to you, it's *my* proposed budget.'"

NEGATIVE SPIN CYCLES

From my stints in St. Charles, Batavia, and Elgin, I'd worked with several very seasoned civil servants—people who were twice my age, people who I admired—who would lecture me, usually in a friendly, well-meaning way, about local government. By and large, they were departmental heads, directors, bureaucrats.

"Here are the things that are impossible in local government, Sean," I'd hear, bracing myself for a litany of negative statements. Here are just a few:

> "You can't raise money for big initiatives without raising taxes, and you can't raise taxes because that is political suicide."
>
> "You can't restructure departments because if things are working well enough, why mess with mediocrity?"
>
> "You can't take risks because failure is another form of political suicide."

"I'm not being a doomsayer," they'd conclude. "I'm just being a realist, Sean. So you can just stop dreaming about these things and save yourself the frustration."

As someone who, by nature, questions authority, my natural response to what I thought of as negative spin cycles was this: "Well, you couldn't do it, but I bet I can."

Was this ego-driven one-upmanship?

The Top of the Arc

These "leaders" were cynical about local government. Part of my enlightenment was that I knew that cynicism is often the by-product of experience. You have to remind people that experiences can differ. As they say in the investment world, past performance is no guarantee of future success—but it is also no guarantee of future failure. That inspired me. Cynicism can be toxic, so you have to actively fight against it. You have to invest in change.

And there was a lot to change.

I'd noticed each town I worked in had many of the same problems. One glaring issue involved accountability, responsibility, and communication. I'd see cop cars driving by tree branches in the parkway and not alerting public works to the road hazard. When I asked why, I was told it was not a safety issue from the police's point of view. Meanwhile, a public works employee might spot someone trespassing in a park at night or selling drugs on the corner and not call the police. And yet, the town government was operating efficiently. Why?

A BRIEF HISTORY OF COUNCIL-MANAGER GOVERNMENT

The Town of Cary is one of 552 municipalities in North Carolina and operates under charters granted by the state's general assembly. All these towns have a municipal charter. The state offers two basic options. The first is a mayor-council government, where the mayor and the council work together to make decisions about services, revenues, and expenditures. Towns can take a slight twist on this setup. It's called the mayor-council with an administrator. The administrator is a sort of utility player who helps the elected officials get over their humps. Cary, however, deploys the second North Carolina municipal governance option: the council-manager form. This empowers the mayor and council to set policy and hire a manager to implement everything. A manager has specified statutory authority, including hiring and firing of employees, with the exception of the town attorney directly and sometimes the clerk. If this last exception recalls the checks and balances at work in the US federal government, well, good. That's the idea.

North Carolina municipal governance laws were enacted in 1971, but ideas behind the council-manager form had been gestating for some time. In 1894, future president Theodore Roosevelt, future Supreme Court justice Louis Brandeis, civil rights activist Mary Munford, and dozens of other leaders gathered at the National Conference for Good City Government in Philadelphia, drawn together by crisis.

American cities were diverse entities that frequently shared similar (and disturbing) traits of corruption, confusion, and dysfunction. Some municipalities were controlled by political machines, such as New York's Tammany Hall, the all-powerful corrupt association that handed out nominations, distributed patronage positions, and collected graft. Others had dictatorial mayors or fragmented districts with dozens of aldermen who answered to party bosses. According to the *National Civic Review*, consistency among towns was a rarity: "Management of municipal departments was fractured across an array of elected or appointed offices, everything from comptroller to dog catcher. Governors and state legislatures interfered freely in local affairs. Lines of accountability were unclear. Waste, inefficiency, and corruption were widespread. Muckrakers such as Lincoln Steffens wrote books with titles like *The Shame of the Cities*."[1]

The conference in Philadelphia marked the founding of the National Civic League,[2] and four years later, it issued its first "Municipal Plan" to give more power and autonomy to local officials, create a city council with nonpartisan elections, and elect a hands-on mayor. Meanwhile, in the town of Staunton, Virginia, the population surpassed 10,000, triggering the commonwealth's mandate to become a bicameral government ruled—or in this case, *not ruled*—by a Board of Aldermen and a common council that refused to work together.

Chaos reigned. As Staunton town historians report, "Each body appointed its own 15 committees. Consequently, each city department reported to two committees, one for each body."[3] Finally, cooler heads prevailed to end the deadlock, and in 1908, Charles E. Ashburner became America's first town manager.

Others noticed. A New York–based social reformer and progressive, Richard S. Childs, heard about Staunton and, convinced that an inefficient and undemocratic government was caused largely by structural deficiencies, began actively advocating for council-manager governments. Eventually, in 1910, he guided the town of Sumter, South Carolina, to hire a manager. Three years later, Dayton, Ohio, a city with a population much larger than either Staunton or Sumter, followed suit. The new form of governance gained steady traction. Now, 115 years after Staunton broke new ground, council-manager local governments abound across America.

In 2021, the National Civic League issued the ninth edition of its *Model City Charter*, which was originally published in 1900. Here's how the updated version describes the city manager job:

> City managers do not just handle the day-to-day operations of city government, as the typical description of the manager's role emphasizes, although this is a crucial contribution. They also manage achieving the long-term goals of the city and provide the council with a professional perspective on the opportunities and challenges that the city faces. Managers are a driving force for innovation and improved performance, and council-manager cities have a stronger record of innovation than mayor-council cities.
>
> Governments are increasingly involved in partnerships to advance their goals, and top administrators must develop strategies to promote their success. . . . Compared to elected officials, managers are uniquely positioned to carry out this function, without the risk that the activity will turn into coalition-building for political purposes.[4]

As job descriptions go, this is pretty inspiring. Managers are a driving force for innovation and improved performance, and council-manager cities have a stronger record of innovation than mayor-council cities. That may be the most uplifting part. But it's also daunting. How do you drive innovation, improve performance, and promote success without playing politics?

SILOS AND SCORN

As an assistant town manager gaining experience and insight, I looked around Elgin's local government and saw staff huddled in bunkers. This, I thought, was the reason behind so much inefficiency—many local governments are siloed. It is—or hopefully, was—the nature of the beast. The fire department, at first blush, has little to do with the sanitation department, right? Actually, wrong. Uncollected garbage is a fire hazard, and its disposal may carry risks. Conversely, fire-training exercises may require coordinated disposals with sanitation experts. These two departments can help each other and, in doing so, serve and safeguard their citizens.

Silos, then, struck me as more likely to breed dysfunction than function. I thought about successful businesses versus local governments. Would Apple or IBM have achieved their stature if they were mired in silos? Every company is made up of divisions: product development, finance, marketing, logistics, IT programming, and customer service. And no doubt, some divisions are more siloed than others. But coordination is the key to any new product launch. And you can bet that when customer service is besieged with calls about missed deliveries, the shipping department is going to hear about it immediately. If a beta test of a new gizmo uncovers issues, delaying a launch, the product development team will be informed quickly, of course, but so will the marketing department promoting the launch. Pretty much every C-suite executive will learn about the issue too, because they will have to deal with the fallout in different ways.

In other words, communication, clarity, trust, and respect are key variables in any large, complex enterprise. Why should publicly traded companies be better at these critical elements of organization than local governments whose entire purpose is to serve the public?

Observing these limitations—poor communication, nonexistent feedback loops, and leaders who are caught in negative spin cycles—bothered me. Speaking of negativity, I also heard a philosophy of contempt (often from people I otherwise respected) about the people we worked with. *There are two types of civil servant: the bosses and the workers. And the workers come in three sizes: barely competent, idiots, or lazy.*

There was that cynicism again. But it was more than that, especially to me, the son of a grocery store clerk and seasonal social worker. It was an ugly, mean, unjustifiable way to view humanity. I didn't buy it.

These prevailing attitudes entrenched the silos. They locked people into accepting a local government as is. I call it surrendering to can't.

You can't fight city hall.

You can't empower change.

You can't improve communication.

You can't help employees become their best selves.

You can't get the council to fund innovation.

Surrendering to can't is a crippling mindset. Sometimes I would try to challenge it with naysaying directors who accused me of being a dreamer.

"Aren't you glad someone dreamed of going to the moon?" I'd ask. "Aren't you glad someone tried to stop the spread of polio?"

In my mind, the naysayers were the ones who made no sense. They didn't believe change was possible, that a ditchdigger could become an enlightened member of the management team, that a town could write its own future. It was misguided, I was told, to think we could. "Sean," I'd hear, "you are being totally naive."

Well, guess what? I will pick naivete over cynicism every day of the week.

I wanted to fix the problems that were so evident, but I wasn't sure how to go about it. How do you stop cynicism? How do you encourage dreams? I didn't have the immediate answers, but it was clear to me that for local governments to win, surrender was not an option.

In 2006, I attended a program at the Kennedy School of Government at Harvard University and took a course about adaptive leadership, and everything changed. As soon as the professor, Marty Linsky, started talking, I experienced my *aha* moment. I saw the light, and the light was building a framework of communication so that people—bosses, workers, citizens, and council members—could confront and solve problems. And that framework was vital to solving a problem that surfaced time and again. Let me lay it out loud and clear.

Human beings and, therefore, their governments are really great at treating symptoms. Preventing those symptoms from surfacing in the first place is another story. We are less than great at that.

Let me give you an example. A number of late, great celebrities—rocker David Crosby, *Dallas* TV star Larry Hagman, and baseball legend Mickey Mantle—all suffered from alcoholism and received liver transplants. Those transplants were amazing medical solutions to clearly lethal problems, since having a functional liver is somewhat essential to staying alive. This particular trio had damaged livers from massive alcohol abuse (and, in the case of Crosby, Hepatitis C), and so the transplant was, in effect, a lifesaving treatment of a severe symptom. The better, commonsense course of action would have been to stop drinking *to prevent the symptoms in the first place*. That was the smart, simple, real solution.

That doesn't mean it was the *easy* solution. Obviously, it takes long-term therapy and medication to treat and overcome addiction. It must have been extremely difficult for Crosby, Hagman, and Mantle—not to mention my own grandfather, who I'll get to in a minute.

But let me finish with my *aha* moment. During my coursework at Harvard, I realized, "I want my life to be spent on real solutions. Kicking the can down the road, settling for mediocrity—it doesn't have to be that way. I want to work on real, effective, impactful solutions."

My professor, Marty Linsky, a coauthor of *Leadership on the Line*, showed me that a framework exists to help people and organizations

The Top of the Arc

introduce change in a way that is substantive and gets people to talk about the "real" issues.

I chose the previous example of liver transplants and alcoholism for a reason. My maternal grandfather died at age 44 of cirrhosis of the liver. You know how hard it is to drink yourself to death at that age? Yet nobody in my family, or in their small community, tried to address the fact that, imprisoned by his disease, he was a raging, self-destructive alcoholic. Part of that, I believe, was because of the social stigma, of the shame of being an addict. It was better to die at age 44 than confront the truth. From what I've learned talking to those who knew him, his family allowed a huge problem to get bigger and bigger because they didn't want to or, for whatever reason, couldn't talk about it.

I like talking about difficult things. In challenging the status quo, questioning people's points of view, and exchanging visions and information, we find where the solutions to problems lie. Not in silence. Not in surrendering to can't.

I returned to Elgin. I continued working with council members, doing my best to help them solve the problems they deemed important while also promoting my own ideas for change. I built relationships. I fought any encounter with people who were surrendering to can't. In 2009, I was promoted to the top job. I saw a new vehicle for change. It was one cities were adopting as a tool to be more efficient. But I thought of it as a more transformational tool. It was and is. And it led me, eventually, to Cary.

CHAPTER 3

COMMUNICATION, GOOD GOVERNANCE, AND 311

If you get nothing else right, get good governance right. Get to know your job and do it well. This is grounded in a commitment to your citizens. I remember serving with a fellow elected official who sat at the Council table and said, "We need to deal with our citizens." And I said, "Citizens aren't people that you 'deal with.' Citizens are people that you serve."

—Jennifer Bryson Robinson, six-term Cary Town Council member

On October 2, 1996, Baltimore launched the first-ever 311 pilot program. The rollout encouraged the city's citizens to dial those three numbers for nonemergency issues to relieve the undue burden on the emergency-only 911 phone number. "Many citizens, unfortunately, use the 911 system to report virtually everything," said County Executive Wayne Curry. "It might be barking dogs. It might be sanitation problems. It might be broken water mains."[1]

The Top of the Arc

This was a serious problem. The phrase *safety first* may have originated to reduce steel industry fatalities, but it embodies a core mission of local government. A town's emergency services—protecting and sustaining the lives of its citizens—should be priority number one.

The abuse of 911 was not just a Baltimore issue. Every day, an average of 260,000 calls asking for help were made to 911 across America, said Curry, "but in most counties, less than half those calls reported life-threatening situations or involved a crime in progress."

Nowadays, most people in large metropolitan areas take 311 for granted. As the first city to embrace this solution, Baltimore had to create an awareness campaign from nothing that stressed dialing 311 for "an urgency but not an emergency." Six months into the initial program, the number of calls to 911 decreased by 20 percent, while calls to the new number climbed. Baltimore officials were understandably pleased. They had found a way to improve their response rates to the people they served.

Across America, 311 programs began to roll out. When I was appointed city manager of Elgin, one of my first promises was to deliver a 311 system. But I didn't want to just throw up a quick fix. I envisioned 311 as a tool that would do far more than alleviate stress on emergency services.

Of course, Elgin's 311 would undoubtedly help 911 operate more efficiently. And it would get citizens better, more responsive service. But that was the low-hanging fruit; every new 311 rollout reported improved response rates. To me, 311 was an opportunity to push Elgin into the future, to ensure better two-way communication with our citizens, to break down silos and unite people. The real power of 311 was serving as a change lever to create new, more sustainable, smarter structures.

That might seem like blue-sky hype. So let me get to specifics.

In 2010, *big data* was becoming a popular term, as was *cloud computing*, which involved linking to a network of remote servers to store, manage, and process data. Governments rely on data for all kinds of decisions and allocations. If a neighborhood reports an increase in vandalism, a police department might increase its presence in the area. If there are water line breaks, public works might be deployed to evaluate plans to ensure continuous service. As I looked at various 311 programs, I felt many cities were putting lipstick on a pig. They were launching 311 on top of archaic systems and declaring victory; they weren't integrating with new technology that was faster and more powerful than anything we'd seen before. Databases? Cloud computing? Customer service management systems? The 311 rollouts I saw were missing the boat.

I had a city to run—one emerging from the 2008 economic crisis. Fortunately, I was under the newfound spell of adaptive leadership, and I found the perfect person to help me modify our culture. His name was Dan Ault, and he was a 24-year-old intern who had earned a full scholarship to get a master's in public administration. Dan had a number of winning qualities. He was very bright, he was tech savvy, he embraced responsibility, he worked his ass off, and he would never surrender to can't.[2]

Of all those qualities, the last may be the most important. It's natural to believe you can change the world when you're young. That is a *good* thing. Because groundbreaking evolution will not occur if everyone in town sticks their head in the sand or if people in silos surrender to can't instead of embracing the ultimate slogan of empowerment: "Just do it."

I told my assistant managers to talk to me about 311. I was interested in hearing what they had to say. Dan Ault, who was barely on the payroll, submitted a 20-page proposal. Nobody else handed in a single paragraph. I shared my vision with Dan. I wanted to find a robust system that could capture data—log incoming calls, communicate with citizens, send updates, let citizens track their requests, and allow us to analyze what the citizens were telling us and how we were performing. Ideally, it would integrate with the town's Oracle-based computer systems. But I realized that compatibility might be an issue.

"Run with it," I said.

He did.

Dan contacted 80 311 centers. He interviewed people who worked on the front line answering phones and talked to senior managers. Some cities were more helpful than others. Several people in Somerville,

The Top of the Arc

Massachusetts, in particular, spent a lot of time on the phone trading insights. In a matter of months, Dan had both micro and macro views about the strengths and weaknesses of 311 systems in operation. Many 311 services had smooth-functioning call centers that connected callers quickly—but the tracking software they used was problematic, requiring jerry-rigging or complicated integration with a local government's computer systems. It was clear that nobody was really working with the kind of flexible platforms that were beginning to populate the digital universe—software-as-a-service enterprise companies that offered plug-and-play platform solutions over the internet. That was what we wanted. But as far as we could tell, nobody was offering it.

We hired a consultant to help issue a request for proposal (RFP) and then sat back and hoped some unheard-of company would surprise us. Dan read through every proposal. He took a deep dive into a solution that would align with Elgin's Oracle software but concluded it lacked the flexibility we wanted. Then he opened up a proposal from Salesforce, a 13-year-old company just hitting its stride that offered cloud-based customer relationship management (CRM) software.

It was a eureka moment. Dan immediately knew this was the platform on steroids that we wanted. Dan is a fast talker normally, but when he showed up with the Salesforce document, he was talking a mile a minute.

"They've proven this works in the private sector," he said. "The only sector they haven't really done it in yet is the public sector. We can be the first. And they need us! Our advantage is that we can be the first to use it. We're going to prove a different model and demonstrate how this can make a difference. And I bet we can get Salesforce to tailor it for us because they need a strong client if they want to break into any other cities."

I trusted Dan. He was born to the native digital generation and understood new paradigms—data, phones, apps, the cloud, and something called edge computing—on an intuitive level that I lacked. Not only that, but he had absorbed a great deal of my thinking and the game theory around adaptive leadership. And if you asked him what the most important element is of strengthening a 21st-century local government—you

Communication, Good Governance, and 311

know, *creating a local government that doesn't exist*—he'd say, "You need new civic infrastructure that facilitates governance in the information age."

Listening to him discuss the flexibility and insight provided by Salesforce's platform, it was clear he thought we'd found the infrastructure we needed.

HOW DATA MANAGEMENT IS A SOFT STAFF MANAGEMENT TOOL

I had said yes to Dan Ault while he was still an intern. Then I hired him as a management analyst and made him the Salesforce implementation and 311 project manager. Was that crazy? Not at all. He had seized the initiative. He was born into the digital culture. He was a great listener and was passionate about the opportunity we had to help Elgin evolve. Having worked closely together in city hall, we were very aligned. Was there a risk in entrusting him to oversee the project? There's risk in everything. Including saying no.

The amazing thing about the work Dan Ault did was that it paid dividends I did not initially expect. It created a new motivational tool: data.

Bear with me on this. Everything will become clear in a moment.

I'm a big proponent of saying yes. Being affirmative and positive is the opposite of surrendering to can't, which people often offer up as a don't-blame-me form of saying no.

As I studied the fine art of leadership and town manager best practices, I realized that my biggest managerial shortcomings involve both saying no and being an accountability cop.

I liked saying yes to my staff. I was a better lifter-upper than a hand-slapper. I didn't like holding my staff accountable and tearing them down when they failed to produce the work expected of them.

How could I confront and adapt my own weaknesses? The answer, I thought, somehow lay in fostering a positive culture of accountability. No doubt, we could put up posters, we could hire coaches, we could incentivize people with bonuses, we could institute quotas and goals and weekly management check-ins. In a rare cynical moment, I imagined monthly self-denunciations like some twisted cultural revolution. No. That was not going to work.

Then it hit me. I realized the vast insight provided by 311, done correctly, would actually make local government and our staff more accountable.

Part of my epiphany was rooted in my playing amateur psychologist. I noticed that one of the great motivators, especially in government, is the fear of public embarrassment. Nobody wants to fail in public. And as you might imagine, project managers and department directors do not want to be called out for nonaccomplishments at town hearings or council meetings.

So the beauty of using a 311 system that can produce and track all manner of data is that it creates a culture of achievement. The system itself, the ability to track data, not only provides answers but also ensures accountability. With 311, I wouldn't have to be the bad guy. I didn't have to be an accountability cop. I just had to parse the data and have the system report back on our performance. Did we respond, did the problem get identified, did it get fixed, and did we follow up with the citizen to make sure the issue was resolved in a satisfactory way? The report tells me whether the town government acquitted itself well or didn't rise to the occasion. And if we didn't, well, then that would be addressed in public.

In chapter 5, I'll delve a bit further into what I call "letting the process say no." But 311, I realized, was a beautiful part of that process. Should anyone accuse me of wielding data like a Big Brother surveillance state to harass workers, let me be clear: that was never and should never be the goal. Developing a 311 call center has many upsides. It should challenge and engage employees, create job diversification, and ideally lead to more satisfying work. Done well, it will also create operational efficiencies, centralize problem-solving, and ultimately help the people we serve.

THE CARY ENGAGEMENT

Elgin launched phase one of its Salesforce-driven 311 service in 2012. The response was instantly gratifying. The town now had a 360-degree view of itself, available to workers and managers. Not only did we have real-time visibility into citizen requests across the city's 19 departments, but those departments could communicate instantly with the citizens of Elgin. They could post status updates. They could send follow-up messages regarding open issues. They could share traffic updates, advise on daily inspections, and post reminders about town meetings and public events.

In March 2015, an independent case study concluded that Elgin had a 120 percent return on investment within seven months of launching 311 and, over a four-year period, reaped an average annual benefit of $553,981.[3] But that undersold the city's success; the authors admitted they hadn't put a price on "the overall enhancements to community-wide communication," and they noted that in the future, "the city will experience additional efficiencies and capabilities as it expands its use of the applications from Salesforce's partner ecosystem with more CRM applications."

That is exactly what happened. Dan brought someone on to create an Elgin mobile app, and we began sending push notifications from Salesforce about traffic incidents such as lane closures. We even developed a regular "Top 3 Things You Need to Know" post. These things served the community and imparted information that would intrinsically improve the quality of life.

Word traveled fast in the 311 community. Elgin began getting inquiries from other towns wanting to learn about what we had done and why. One of those inquiries came from the Town of Cary's chief information officer, Nicole Raimundo, and in February 2016, Dan and I traveled to Cary to share what we'd learned. In the process, we also learned about Cary.

The Top of the Arc

That's not to say Cary was a complete mystery to me. I had driven through the town many times on my way to North Carolina beach vacations with my family over the years. And for someone interested in local government, Cary was a hard town to miss, given its annual presence on best-of surveys and articles. But when Dan and I got here, we heard that the local government didn't have any glaring performance issues. Unlike Baltimore and Elgin and so many other municipalities that turned to 311, Cary wasn't overwhelmed with complaints. The town, befitting its reputation for quality-of-life excellence, provided exceptional service to its citizens. Everything was under control.

So why were we here?

A few reasons emerged. The town knew its departments were siloed. Each department had a separate phone number and its own process for tracking public requests. Although there were few complaints about departmental responses, the data about received requests, as well as other departmental information, could not be centralized due to incompatible computer systems. We also discovered that departments didn't actually track calls in which answers were immediately provided. This was a glaring data collection no-no. Just because an interaction was resolved quickly doesn't mean it didn't happen. Perhaps there was something the government could do to prevent that call in the first place.

As for calls that came into one department that were actually the responsibility of another office, well, that was not an infrequent problem. When it occurred, it could sometimes mutate into an annoying game of well-meaning but frustrating "hot potato," with emails and phone calls passing from one office to another, hoping to find the right person who could address the initial call.

Meanwhile, if a call came in that required a division like solid waste or public works to "roll a truck," a work order was written up and printed out. Remember, this was 2016—email had been in existence for a quarter of a century. Smart devices with email capability, like the BlackBerry, had been around for 17 years. But Cary was tracking its work in old-school triplicate.

Communication, Good Governance, and 311

The town also realized it had to update some of its systems. For example, the 20-year-old case management system used by the Cary Department of Public Works was about to be discontinued. The department searched for a replacement management system. It found specialized software to manage water accounts, to track sewage treatment, to manage inventory and operations needs. But all these tools required separate installations, separate databases, separate passwords. They couldn't easily talk to each other. In other words, the available replacement systems would silo information; 311 should integrate these tasks to operate within a larger system.

Perhaps the biggest motivating factor was something felt but not quite articulated. Something every department saw looming on the horizon: Imagine Cary, the road map that pointed to the future. The Town Council was moving toward finalizing the Cary Community Plan. If Cary was going to grow and evolve, what was the digital infrastructure, the operating system, that would serve as both the brain and heart to drive everything forward?

That led to a series of equally critical questions. What did the town want to achieve by doing this? What would the impact of such a system be? How would such a system influence the local government? There were endless attendant questions about incorporating a 360-degree management tool. Would jobs change? Would departments change? Would an old-school manager—someone, say, unfamiliar with social media—need to become a digital know-it-all overnight?

These were big issues and great questions. They needed answers. Someone showed me the Cary Community Plan, and I thought, "This is a town with its eyes on the prize."

In every department of every local government, change or the mere discussion of change inevitably leads to uncertainty. I was fully aware of this phenomenon. It's a fundamental tenet of adaptive leadership. As Dan and I talked to members of the Cary government about 311 and the Salesforce platform, we described the powerful potential of tracking every interaction. Of how efficient the system was. Of how it would foster connectivity, accountability, and unforeseen possibilities. Seriously, Salesforce was in the business of helping clients help themselves; we had no idea what new game-changing features they might add to the platform.

We also stressed that introducing such a tool and getting the desired implementation right would require intense planning and strategic thinking. One of the first critical steps to ensuring that happened meant getting the buy-in from the people who would use it the most.

At the risk of stating the obvious, our presentation went over well. Two months later, in May 2016, Cary procured its first licenses from Salesforce. I was hired in August as town manager and tasked with leading the implementation of 311.

Not long ago, a Cary employee who'd been working for the town for 20 years when I was hired explained to a Cary newcomer why I got the job. Here's what was said: "Sean arrived on the heels of decades of sitting town managers who were cut from the same cloth. They all knew each other and had followed the same path: they joined the government, became the assistant manager, and then, when their boss moved on, they became the manager. It was rinse and repeat. By and large, they were very similar—very calm, very North Carolina, very traditional managers.

"The Cary 2040 Plan said it wanted to make Cary more urban. And that meant we really needed to become something that we weren't. We realized we needed to become a better version of an urban town like Elgin. But we didn't know how to do it. We didn't have the experience. So Sean's experience, in addition to being a change agent, fit in at just the right time to start us on the evolution."

BEST PRACTICE, BEST IMPLEMENTATION

There are many ways managers can lift people up—kind words in private, public commendations, simply saying hello, asking a personal (but not intrusive) question, giving people promotions, approving a raise,

Communication, Good Governance, and 311

or bestowing more responsibility on a team member because they've earned it.

Lifting people up can be reciprocal. I enjoy helping people. It makes me feel good. As town manager, I also rely on my staff. There is no way in the world I, or anyone, am equipped to micromanage a town of 190,000 or 19,000 or even 1,900. So I have to rely on my staff to lift me up. To help me be a better manager. I cannot and do not do it alone.

With that in mind, after barely being on the job for just a few months, I brought Dan Ault to Cary, adding him to the existing ranks of assistant town managers but creating the new second title of chief innovation officer. If we were going to optimize 311 using Salesforce, nobody in America had more experience mining the platform's CRM technology and applying it to civic issues. Given that, you might expect that I wanted Dan to start pushing the process forward. I did, and so did he. But we both knew that effective organic adaptation doesn't happen at the crack of a whip and that changing technology implicitly changes culture. Adaptive change advocates warn about moving too far too fast. As *Leadership on the Line* advises, "Raising issues before they are ready to be addressed, you create an opportunity for those you lead to sideline both you and the issue. You need to wait until the issue is ripe, or ripen it yourself."

Instead of issuing directives, Dan attended meetings, met the vast Cary team, listened, and took the temperature of the many different rooms he entered. When it felt right, he began talking about 311. He described some of the strengths and capabilities of the Salesforce platform. He invited questions. The strategy was part Aesop ("Slow and steady wins the race"), part Hippocratic oath ("I will do no harm"), and definitely part adaptive leadership. "I took several years of learning and studying 311, and you can't shortcut all of that," Dan said. "So an important element was pace. Organizationally, so many things had to ripen culturally for us."

Most Americans have no idea that the Association of Government Contact Center Professionals exists or that it holds an annual conference. The organization's very existence shows, on one level, how much 311 has changed the public sector landscape. However, in 2018, a group from

Cary attended the AGCCP event and found that little had changed in terms of comprehensive solutions since I'd first become interested in 311. There was no out-of-the-box software platform that would serve as the backbone to connect with the public, track any and all issues internally, and collect data in a flexible manner.

"It turned out that what we wanted to build here, what we were imagining here, was this unicorn," said Carolyn Roman, Cary's public information supervisor who was on the 311 planning team. "It didn't exist anywhere else. We found that a lot of folks just try to merge people physically in a room together, but they don't address the processes."

IMAGINING A UNICORN AND BUILDING IT ARE TWO DIFFERENT THINGS

In 2018, I approved an eight-month 311 pilot program, hoping we were ready to mold a civic-minded, problem-solving unicorn into shape. Our call center team using the Salesforce operating system were called citizen advocates. I loved the term. Right up front, we had succeeded in framing the 311 engagement paradigm. Citizens would call. The people who helped them were, logically, citizen advocates. The rest of the implementation was not as seamless. I won't dig into all the growing pains, like finding a space for 311 to exist, recruiting employees to volunteer to work limited hours as citizen advocates (essentially creating a new job that didn't exist), and then training advocates on a vast array of issues. This last challenge was brutal. Understanding the minutiae of a town, from recycling rules to water bills to town permit applications, is a full-time job; it was absurd to expect that a skeleton crew could absorb it. We also learned that the case intake page advocates used—which was initially built for public works to document all calls—was not going to work for a town-wide service.

In hindsight, that last issue probably seems obvious. But that speaks to the huge scope of what we were doing and the sort of free-for-all, open-ended process of our initial development system.

The pilot was bumpy. But we learned a lot. We needed a dedicated team to ensure a launch within a year. Having shaken up the status quo, we needed to calm the chaos that inevitably followed. We needed clear-cut project management to address open issues and focus the staff. Dan Ault came to me and said that to ensure Cary could cope with its mandate, he needed a dedicated team. We created a research and development division and assigned a core group to help launch 311. With responsibility, ideally, comes clarity. And after years of learning, the clouds began to part. The 311 team developed a systematic plan to gradually migrate Cary's three siloed old-school call centers for public works, finance/utility billing, and inspections and permits into our new centralized program. It also forged an agreement for a universal, one-document-fits-all intake page for citizen requests. We started interviewing for full-time citizen advocates so they would have time to learn their jobs.

CHAPTER 4
CULTURAL CHANGE AND ADAPTING TO COCREATION

They feel like they can have an idea, and that can become what they do. That's the thing I hear most from staff. They feel if they have an idea, it could be what Cary does, if they voice it, and it gets talked through. That's great to hear. "Leadership at all levels," I think, is the best phrase for it, and that's not easy to do. You have to actively, every day, come into the town campus, and everybody has to live that. It's very difficult. And I think everyone's bought into it, and everybody does that. So that's the biggest thread in the culture.
—Carissa Kohn-Johnson, first-term Cary Town Council member

When I arrived in Cary from Elgin and met with the town government staff, I said, "There are 1,200 of you, and there's one of me. And I will lose if all of you don't cocreate this culture with me."

This wasn't just team-building lip service on my part. I believe collaborative governance is the core of good governance. Our society loves

Cultural Change and Adapting to Cocreation

to glorify leaders. The world wants its heroes—in sports, in Marvel movies, in business, and yes, even in politics.

The idea that one person can be the hero who saves us all is a fantastic narrative—both as in "It's a great story" and "That is, um, fantasy." Since the demigods of Marvel's universe aren't going to materialize off-screen any time soon, we will have to find our heroes, our leaders, elsewhere. As for sports heroes, they do exist on-screen and off. But at the risk of being a killjoy, it's worth noting that in team sports, an individual "superstar" performer may rescue a team or win a game, but they are always part of a larger entity. As for "individual" sports, runners, cyclists, and tennis stars don't exist in a vacuum; they have coaches, trainers, masseuses, teammates, and sponsors too. So most star athletes are talented cogs in a complex machine. It's the same in business and politics. Leaders are part of the machine. The best can serve as an engine, driving an organization forward and providing energizing inspiration by communicating vision and strategy. Or, to continue the metaphor, they can act as an axle, ensuring alignment. But leaders don't do anything single-handedly, and the best ones don't try to. They do just the opposite. Great leaders don't micromanage; they collaborate, orchestrate, and put people in positions to excel.

And guess what? Invested, engaged, and challenged cocreators end up micromanaging themselves. Or should I say, micrococreating?

My point during that early Cary meeting wasn't to issue a warning; it was to encourage a new mindset. I meant what I said: new undertakings would only succeed with a new culture rooted in collaboration. Cocreation was the approach we needed to capitalize on to enact positive change and growth—which is what towns and cities need to do to survive and thrive.[1]

I was trying to get everyone to buy in. To collaborate and cocreate together. (I know that's redundant—you can't really collaborate alone, can you?—but I like the unifying emphasis of *together*.)

Buying into cocreation is a funny expression, at least to me. Generally speaking, I think there's a big difference between buying in and cocreation, and I try to be hyperaware of distinguishing between the two. An example of buying in would involve a CEO trying to persuade or cajole a board or a staff to adopt a detailed, self-authored, cut-and-dried vision to improve the bottom line without asking for input from others. (You know: "I've got a vision to save the company! We're going to cut staff 15 percent and raise prices 10 percent—starting last week!") Conversely, cocreation would involve saying, "Hey, I've got the outline of what I think we can or should do. Now let's write the chapters together and figure out what the optimal outcome should be."

Building things together—whether it's a road map for the future, a new 311 service, or a school fundraiser—is true cocreation. I like saying, "Go, here are the keys! Move ahead!" I want my staff to study cutting-edge proposals, explore innovative ideas, and come back with a new paradigm, product, or process. Present it. Critique it. Learn. Iterate. Create.

That invitation is much more compelling than asking a group to buy into an idea they had nothing to do with. A single concept emanating from one person is unlikely to match the power or sustainability of cocreation. That's because cocreation is closer to co-ownership. It makes participants more invested in the process and the outcome. They embrace responsibility not just because they will be accountable to themselves but because they are accountable to their collaborators. All these motivations coalesce to make participants more invested in a given project—and invested citizens are perhaps the most potent tool in creating good government.

311 IN SLO-MO REPLAY, PART 1

I had already seen Cary's invested citizens in action when I learned about the Imagine Cary initiative and then watched the Town Council pass the resulting inspirational manifesto. It demonstrated that the town was already trying to create a local government that did not exist—before I got here.

I want to return to 311. Readers may have noticed a kind of elephant in the room. From a certain perspective, Cary's 311 launch was a painful,

Cultural Change and Adapting to Cocreation

overlong, iterative mess. And since Dan Ault and I had created 311 with Salesforce years earlier in Elgin, a reasonable question lurked in those pages: Why did it take so long to reconfigure and deploy in Cary?

There are several answers. The first two that leap to mind are simple overviews. It was a bumpy ride, first and foremost, because we were trying to cocreate without actually dictating. And that leads to the second answer. We wanted to change the culture and instill adaptive leadership practices, hoping they would become embedded in Cary's DNA. The traditional, all-too-common dictatorial behavior of town management needed to evolve into a collaborative process.

There is a catch to all this, however. While people say they want change, they find that living through that change is often difficult. Why? First, the idea of change comes with a distant but constant cousin: the possibility of failure. Second, when things start happening quickly, when people feel that things are moving fast, they get scared. *What if this isn't what we want? What if we were duped? What if there are unintended consequences?*[2]

As a town manager, I don't want anyone to get scared or feel like something the town is doing is dangerous. A town manager seeks to reduce any fear factor. So moving fast, or creating the impression of moving too fast, is not a best practice. With a project like 311, it was clear that we would have to upend entrenched systems and jobs and even divisions of the town government. Dan and I knew it. But it was important for the workers to discover it for themselves and figure out how to turn change into opportunities—without feeling rushed.

How do you do that?

THE SLOW PLAY AND THE RULE OF THREE

Slow playing is a betting strategy in poker deployed by card players with strong hands. Instead of betting aggressively and intimidating competitors into folding, a player with three aces, for example, bets timidly until

The Top of the Arc

the final round. Then, as the final wagers are placed, they suddenly bet big and, ideally—boom!—take the pot.

I realize a poker reference in a book about good governance may seem odd. But in this case, it's appropriate. Every project a town takes on has an element of risk. You may achieve what you set out to do, or you may fail. Or, quite often, you may fall somewhere on that spectrum. If we view change as having inherent risk, how do you keep change from moving too fast and upping the fear factor? This is where the casual manner of the slow play is helpful, and it leads me to another catchphrase: the rule of three.

When introducing new ideas or initiatives to Council members or our staff for the first time, I try to be very low-key. I do this intentionally because downplaying or slow playing a new idea can produce instant returns. Even when I'm not doing a hard sell, I can learn from the responses. If someone reacts positively—"That's an amazing idea. Let's do it!"—I may conclude we are onto something. But if they say, "I don't know, Sean. I'm not too sure about this," I can consider my initial remark a trial balloon that might not be worthy of liftoff.

The second time I broach the subject—especially with Council members—I morph into the role of a casual but purposeful messenger. "Hey, remember that initiative we talked about?" I ask. "We're really starting to do some work on it. So we're getting closer to the point where I'm going to ask you to make a decision." I assume this approach because, having been casual the first time, I might not have connected at all. My initial comment might have not registered or might have gone in one ear and out the other. This second time, I'm being informative and matter-of-fact, but I need to come away convinced that the Council or team member has received the message.

That's because the next step—the third time I bring the topic up—is basically the final notice. I'm letting the Council member or staffer or group know that decision time is now on the calendar and approaching in the near future: "Hey, I don't need to know right now, but I am going to need to know soon." As town manager, I may have a definite opinion or desired outcome for the decision—usually, I do. But often,

Cultural Change and Adapting to Cocreation

I send a message with my final notice: whatever happens, happens. "If you change your mind over the weekend and decide you don't want to approve a measure, it's not a big deal," I say. "It will be fine. Some people might be frustrated. But that's just part of the process. It is your job to make these calls. So really: Do. Not. Worry."

I mean that. Council members, committee members, and department directors have been empowered to make decisions. Sometimes, the pressure to make those decisions can feel immense. That's why my slow-play rule of three serves three purposes:

1. I want to take the pressure off as much as possible. Sometimes if the pressure builds, people hit the eject button. They blow up the very thing they have been focusing on.
2. I aim to apply an empowering form of reverse psychology. If you constantly let people know that they can bail at any moment—which is a way of expressing that they are in control of the situation and not being forced into anything—they often won't. Similarly, when you tell people something is not a big deal, they may become more relaxed and effective because you have reduced stress.
3. Finally and most importantly, laying out a proposal slowly promotes thoroughness, which is essential to good governance. The Cary Town Council decisions don't belong to me. They belong to the Council and they belong to the citizens of Cary. But I have to set them up to make sure the Council can evaluate an issue and every member can be heard, and that can and should take time. A town manager, then, can take ownership over the process by which things get decided, but not the actual decisions themselves. Those decisions, those votes—they are taken care of by something called democracy.

The Top of the Arc

311 IN SLO-MO REPLAY, PART 2

When Dan Ault arrived in Cary, he was surprised that so many people were eager to use Salesforce as the backbone of 311. "Everyone has drunk the Salesforce Kool-Aid," he recalled. But this made sense. The town explored new platforms, and they saw how Elgin deployed 311 and came away impressed.

That was great from a buy-in standpoint but not from a cocreation standpoint. Cary was not Elgin, and vice versa. We needed to ensure we broke new ground. One of the challenges of integrating a new system is guarding against what I like to call "inherent anti-innovation creep." This is an insidious problem in which old solutions are integrated into new technology. To prevent this, you need to combat conventional wisdom counterintuitively. Let me give you an example. Typically and logically, a vendor with new technology might interview all the departments that will use the new technology. And just as logically, these departments will tell the vendor what they need. This can very easily result in the vendor using new technology to configure a new system that is very similar to the old system. Instead of building a robust new paradigm, you've created a legacy system 2.0.

We didn't want that to happen with Salesforce and Cary. We wanted the town to figure out best practices—to develop an optimized, efficient, new information and communication infrastructure.

But it is very difficult to imagine something when faced with a blank slate. You can ask people to imagine new communications paradigms, but those first-pass ideas will likely be underwhelming. People need inspiration or something to respond to.

"It's the number-one mistake every city makes," Dan said, having had years to reflect on implementation processes. "And I'm including Cary; we've made it several times. You can't just ask people to dream up future infrastructure. You have to give people something to react to. And you have to do it step by step by step with people-first values."

Cultural Change and Adapting to Cocreation

I appreciate Dan's last point. As 311 unfolded, it became clear that the new paradigm would affect the lives of our town government staff. We were disassembling and reconfiguring three well-oiled customer service departments into a new division, aiming to use technology to elevate efficiency and redefine the roles of our employees. But we weren't just messing with bureaucracy; we were impacting people's jobs and, by extension, their lives.

This led to a circular irony: We were building a new system to give the town and government access to more information to make better decisions. But because it hadn't been built yet, we didn't have access to the information we needed to make better decisions that would affect our employees' jobs and lives. This is where our efforts got a little messy. We needed to try things, reject things, switch things. We needed to test and, yes, fail. Before that, we needed to agree on what we were trying, rejecting, and testing.

Making those determinations required forming committees, hours and hours of meetings, active listening, and even more active analysis. As the initiative took shape, many questions had to be asked about how the new enterprise would impact the current organizational structure of the Cary government. For example, if 311 was about collecting and disseminating information, how would that change the role of the Department of Communication? Or, if we were melding three existing call centers, what would happen to the employees who staffed those departments, and who, exactly, would become the citizen advocates who would serve as the faces and voices of 311?

One staffer who worked on the 311 pilot planning committee, Carolyn Roman, had spent nine years working in our Communications Department and already endured a name change from the Public Information Office. When she signed up to join the planning committee, I'm not sure she realized she would be contributing to what might, eventually, feel like the demise of her department. But because she was part of the process, she understood the larger picture.

"I felt like as my involvement ramped up at 311 that I was losing more [of the] PIO [Public Information Office], and that was really hard because that's why I came to the town," she said. "Even as we were going through the pilot, I had to remind myself that what we're doing is more than a call center. It's a gigantic infrastructure of information."

Carolyn wasn't alone in her feelings of loss. A postmortem report of the 311 launch found others who joined the pilot and felt guilty about abandoning their former departments.

All of these types of emotions are to be expected during the cocreation process. But being part of the journey adds perspective, insight, and ideally, excitement and inspiration to balance the difficulty of such transitions. As the authors of *Leadership on the Line* put it, "To persuade people to give up the love they know for a love they've never experienced means convincing them to take a leap of faith in themselves and in life. They must experience the loss of a relationship that, despite its problems, provides satisfaction and familiarity, and they will suffer the discomfort of sustained uncertainty about what will replace it."[3]

In the end, the Communications Department was dissolved at the same time 311 launched. These were traumatic events. But in hindsight, the changes have been positive. Carolyn spent two years as Cary's services design coordinator and is now the assistant director of 311, managing the department she helped build. I'm also happy to report that we worked very hard to find new fits for displaced staff. Jobs evolved. Remember, we launched in 2020, when there were members of the public works team who didn't have email accounts. Now many of these people have iPads and have increased their digital skills.

UNANTICIPATED BENEFITS

Let me return to the elephant in the room. Yes, cocreation can feel scary, sloppy, and inefficient.

The larger effect, however, is that it leads to all kinds of evolution. Organizations change, and the people who provide the foundation of those organizations will change too—by necessity, by desire, by the momentum of the process. It is incumbent on leaders to stir things up,

Cultural Change and Adapting to Cocreation

provide encouragement, and remain allies to the people who fuel the organization—even when chaos looms. Learning from mistakes can be just as valuable as confirming an initial hunch. Two full-blown implementations of 311 later, I'm aware of legacy creep. I know it helps to provide rudimentary baselines when asking old hands for new ideas. I understand that the most common intake form is not going to work for every issue. And I know that people are going to be scared about their jobs changing or even ending.

Speaking of chaos and termination, I want to sound a cautionary note. Not everyone is built to cocreate. And some employees will need help with certain evolutions. Change is imperfect. One of the strengths of cocreation is that it can identify preferences, weaknesses, and vulnerabilities. As we rolled out 311, it became clear that some call center workers did not want to be citizen advocates and preferred micro-problem-solving to 311's macro agenda. Some employees decided they were too old to evolve. Organizations should anticipate these reactions and factor them into planning. They should offer lateral opportunities as well as promotions. And to facilitate those promotions, they must be willing to invest time and money into helping employees learn new skills.

Most of all, they should stress opportunity and positivity. If new skill sets are required, that's a *good thing*. The employee becomes more skilled, empowered, and valuable. They benefit. But so does the collective. Organizations are cocreating new, more dynamic, more impactful citizens who can use their power to cocreate the government that doesn't exist.

That is the ultimate dividend.

CHAPTER 5

GETTING THE CULTURE RIGHT

THE ONECARY TOOLKIT

It is important that we care about those with means as much as we care for those in need. We need to be in a position to help everyone as much as possible.
—Michelle Craig, first-term Cary Town Council member

As we've just seen, cocreation can be messy and complicated, especially for organizations that are new to the concept. But cocreating is more than just an idea. It's a verb, an action. It's something local governments *do* and benefit from. Therefore, it must be fostered and integrated into organizational culture from the top down and the ground up.

Before we get to how that can be achieved, let me share, again at the risk of stating the obvious, a fundamental truth. Every town seeking to create a government that doesn't exist will deploy the same building blocks: people. Government simply doesn't work without them—it should be, as Abe Lincoln eloquently stated, "of the people, by the people, for the people."

Getting the Culture Right

Lincoln, of course, was focusing on national unity and "the new birth of freedom" when he delivered those words in the Gettysburg Address (a mere 88 years *before* Dr. Elliott Jaques first wrote about the concept of organizational culture in 1951). But as it happens, unity and its cousin solidarity are critical tenets of effective local government. A heavily divided community, a polarized town council, or even a fractured municipal department will have difficulty making constructive, beneficial decisions. Additionally, unity can operate as the antithetical force to combat silos. If people and departments are working in different bunkers, how can they cocreate? Governments need to establish a nurturing, respectful environment—a culture—in which all our primary building blocks, people, flourish without fear or favor.

Cary already had a strong, functioning culture before I arrived. But to achieve the ambitious, inspiring goals laid out in the Imagine Cary Community Plan, the town's culture needed to evolve too. If we were going to build up the town, we needed to build up the staff. The town government needed a vision and language, a process, a supportive network to help us ensure that good works become great. In a sense, the Imagine Cary Community Plan name dictated what we needed to pay attention to: *community*. With all the technical, physical change that was coming, my concern was how to ensure we kept what was precious to Cary while also evolving into a more resilient, flexible, people-focused government. All of which is to say, I felt we had to get Cary's culture right. Otherwise, evolving to achieve the ambitious, inspiring goals laid out in the Imagine Cary Community Plan would be extremely problematic, if not impossible.

When a town or city is making huge decisions about projects that require millions of dollars, tens of millions of dollars, or even hundreds of millions of dollars, it needs to have shared values in place. People must have an underlying respect for each other, the town, and the process. And they need to let that process—the discovery, the innovation, the feedback loops, the data, the respect for stated goals, *the very culture itself*—steer toward positive outcomes. And sometimes, that positive outcome will involve rejecting ideas. This is what I mean about "letting the process say no." It can be frustrating when that happens. But ideally and optimally, the culture underpins all the things that local government can accomplish.

CULT OR CULTURE?

Part of the evolving culture I envisioned for Cary required the open exchange of ideas. I wanted that for my staff and for our government departments. I also wanted that for myself. But I also knew the exchanges could not be exclusively with insiders. That's because, while unity is important, unity without introspection and external perspectives is dangerous. When a town pursues an open exchange of ideas, it will benefit from seeking input from outside sources. As the leader of Cary's government operations, I have sought out people who study leadership and organizations to help me be better at my job.

One sounding board I found was Diana Hong, a communications and leadership expert at CRA Inc., a leading consulting firm. In an early exchange, she said, "There's a very slight difference between a cult and a culture. A cult requires its charismatic leader to be there. And when the charismatic leader isn't there, it doesn't work. It falls apart or fades. A culture lasts no matter who's in the room. It carries itself. And so what I want to ask you, Sean, is, What are you building, a culture or a cult?"

Recently, Diana recounted this story to a friend, stressing that I answered, "Culture, of course!" She then added, "I think our work together has really been about how you translate all of the things that make Sean great and charismatic and compelling as a leader, everything from his genuine care about people to his honest, forthright manner. How do you translate that into an organization so that it stays whether or not he's in the room?"

As flattering and kind as Diana's quote is, I'm not sharing this to toot my own horn. I'm sharing it to focus on her question about creating an effective organization. It's a question that any town manager or leader would want to solve because running an organization that thrives 24/7 is what we aspire to. The short answer, for me, was culture. The longer answer was to emulate the culture I wanted to build by asking my colleagues for their input. And that is precisely what I did.

Sort of.

ONECARY

The first colleague I asked to help codify and teach a new Cary culture was Allison Hutchins, who had spent the previous two years as assistant to the town manager for my predecessor. On paper, Allison was impressive; she had a master's in public administration and had worked as a senior advisor to a US Treasury official in DC. She was even more remarkable in person: analytical, ambitious, committed to excellence and government as a force for good. When she shared that she relocated back to the Triangle when her father fell ill, I was not at all surprised. She was clearly a passionate, people-first person.

In addition to staking out the launch of 311, I announced the formation of the Department of Learning and Organizational Development—launched with Allison and Kathryn Trogdon, a former journalist who was part of the Cary communications team.

It was a tough job for several reasons. First, Allison and Kathryn had to learn about me and understand my thoughts about culture and adaptive leadership. This was difficult because although I aspire to be a better listener than a talker, I have the gift of gab too—my grandmother said I could trade stories with Aesop. That meant they had to absorb my ideas about developing the Cary government and the people in that government. The second part of their mission was figuring out how to shape those ideas in an articulate way that would explain where we had come from and how our culture would take us someplace new. I needed help communicating how Cary was going to evolve as a town and how our government would evolve too.

The Top of the Arc

Explaining or framing the "old Cary way" was essential to me because it provided a celebratory baseline from which we could move forward. Since we knew change—evolution—was our future, it would be helpful for people to recognize what we were changing *from*. When people go on unfamiliar journeys, they consult books and maps. They look at websites and read the impressions of other people who have gone before them. They do that to feel more comfortable about the path they are taking and to acclimate themselves to a new environment.

Cary was going on a journey. I wanted a map and guidebook that would address the issues we were destined to encounter and reassure people that we understood where they were coming from and recognized the great work they had done. I hoped articulating that would make people more comfortable; providing a common launching point makes the journey forward feel less dangerous or threatening.

Fortunately, Allison agreed with all this.

"People want something concrete to hold on to," she told me, adding that she thought the organization wanted a map and definitions even more than I did. "Not everybody understands the distinctions, especially about defining the 'old Cary way.'"

Allison and Kathyrn also collaborated extensively with Renee Poole, Cary's chief of human resources, and together, they worked with a team at CRA to put all these thoughts on paper. Somewhere along the way, two concepts began to take root. The first involved creating a tool kit—a document that would do more than codify our values. It would also literally provide tools—in the form of best practices and questions and answers—to help people solve issues that might emerge with this new paradigm.

The second was that I mentioned a nugget from my past. In my oversharing way, I said I had thought of all the culture-building work I'd done in my previous job as "OneElgin." Allison, proving she was an excellent critical listener, picked up on the anecdote and ran with it.

Or as she explains, "We were focusing on interdepartmental collaboration and the need to break down silos to operate effectively as one organization serving Cary, hence OneCary."

It sounds simple, but there was a lot of trial and error involved in defining the document. Renee remembers the challenges: "How do we take something like this—a statement about values and best practices—and talk to employees about it? We talked about Sean's style, and how we had our legacy, and then how we brought that to the cocreation of our culture with a future Cary plan.

"We had to work at taking all these ideas, all these things that Sean's bringing, and keep what's precious, and then actually make it something that people would connect to and understand—that would be meaningful to everyone on the executive team all the way to a police officer, a firefighter, or our solid waste collectors. It had to be something that everyone could connect to no matter where they were. And if not, it would be a failure. So there were many times that we tried something, but it didn't work, and we tried something else."

In other words, articulating and codifying Cary government values and culture was—surprise!—messy and time-consuming. But eventually, the team's efforts paid off. The OneCary Toolkit was an impressive document. Let me share how the overview begins (see figure 5.1).

The simple Venn diagram in figure 5.1 conveys how our past, present, and future intersect. And overlapping circular rings echoed, at least to me, the interlocking rings of the Olympic logo, which also underscores unity—or in our case, a unified vision. The verbal elements were equally important, articulating the key values of the culture we envisioned. It was all there: Cary's decades of passionate devotion to excellence, the ideas I believed were vital to good governance, and the essential elements that would propel us to cocreate a government that did not exist.

Allison and Renee envisioned the tool kit as an evolving project, one that would require revisiting, refining, and updating. The first iteration of the OneCary Toolkit had five sections: "Our Story," "Leading through Change," "Frequently Asked Questions," "Example Scenarios," and "Additional Resources." Part of me wants to share the entire document, but since we copyrighted it, I'll summarize and excerpt the highlights.

The Top of the Arc

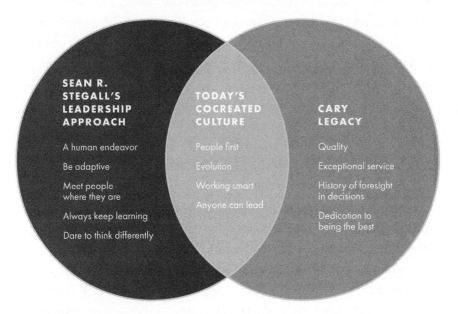

Figure 5.1. Sean R. Stegall's leadership approach, combined with the excellent citizen service that sets Cary apart, helped develop the cocreated culture the organization has today.

"Our Story" explains the vision of Cary and the purpose of the document. Doing that required distilling Cary's mission, values, and purpose. So we cited challenging and reimagining the standard for local government as our mission. Our primary vision involved the following:

- Enhancing lives through diversity
- Bringing the community together to solve public problems
- Implementing the Imagine Cary Community Plan

And our purpose—our reason for being—was to build on Cary's legacy of excellence by challenging convention and partnering effectively with our community to demonstrate that our local government was a committed partner and trusted steward of community resources.

Getting the Culture Right

The section ends by restating the OneCary values at the center of the Venn diagram. Here are the bullet points:

- **People First:** We exist to build an inclusive community and take care of people.
- **Evolution:** We seize opportunities to experiment, learn, and adapt to create a better future.
- **Working Smart:** We prioritize work on the most important things.
- **Anyone Can Lead:** We differentiate leadership from authority and believe that everyone can find ways to make our community better.[1]

Reading these over, I'm struck by how hard we worked to define rather simple concepts. I mean, really, two of these are no-brainers. Why else should government exist if not to take care of its people, right? And should you prioritize *unimportant over important* things? This is common sense. Yet it needs to be said.

Meanwhile, there are two ideas that are not exactly obvious but are innovative in their own way. Evolution is scary to some people. Therefore, change needs to be portrayed positively. More radical is the idea that anyone can lead. An essential tenet of adaptive leadership, this is an empowering idea in many ways, which is why it is perhaps the core value underpinning Cary culture. It underscores equity, possibility, teamwork, and unity. It encourages innovation and adaptation because it invites people to embrace responsibility in every job at every level of government.

New ideas require new levels of clarity. And the next section of the tool kit, "Leading through Change," aimed to provide just that with a series of statements and instructions that instill concepts of adaptive leadership. A friend has told me that, taken out of context, the blurbs resemble "text art" or short poems. That may be true, but within the tool kit, they function as commonsense adages about daily life and maintaining a thoughtful, positive, always-learning mindset. They are principles

The Top of the Arc

for getting from point A to point B and guidelines for leading *during* that process.

Here are some favorites:

WE RESERVE THE RIGHT TO
GET SMARTER AS WE GO.

THINGS WILL HAPPEN THAT
WE CAN'T PREDICT.

HOW WE COMMUNICATE
IS IMPORTANT.

COMMUNICATE GOOD
NEWS REGULARLY.

I admire all nine of the adages. But I think this one conveys the essence of good governance most clearly:

WE STAND FOR TRANSPARENCY.
Be honest about the facts, even if they are going to be
perceived unfavorably. When people are surprised,
they may respond emotionally.

This isn't so much an adaptive trait. Or one about change. It's about the honesty, trust, and communication that underpin all effective leadership and cocreation. Dishonesty, mistrust, and silence breed disunity. This entry also, albeit indirectly, plays into the idea I have talked about regarding data and process. Looked upon with open minds, the data and the process of evaluating the data serve as good-governance maps; they are the guides we need to move us forward, to tell us yes or no.

Guidelines for a journey are helpful. Specifics, however, are also necessary. Your fellow travelers will have questions: "What is allowed?" and

"What is expected of me?" And of course, the ever-present "What is not allowed?" and "Why is it not allowed?" So the longest, most detailed section of the tool kit presents "Frequently Asked Questions." Here are some highlights:

> ### (?) Can I Speak Up about Something I Disagree With?
>
> **Answer:** Cary employees are encouraged to bring their whole self to work, including their experiences, perspectives, cultures, etc. Sharing your thoughts and ideas could lead the organization toward more innovative and effective ways of doing business. For each idea, the path forward may vary, but your colleagues, supervisor, and talent and culture consultants are all avenues for gathering feedback. While we understand that being vulnerable can sometimes be challenging, vulnerability is vital to the success of our organization because it fosters trust, understanding, and compassion among one another.

> ### (?) What Is a Smart Failure and Why Are They Important?
>
> **Answer:** A smart failure is when you are able to learn something from a failed experiment. Smart failures are crucial for us to continue improving how we do business and get smarter as we go. Yet despite the possibility of failure, it is important that experiments still be well thought out to ensure that valuable learning is gained from the experience.

The Top of the Arc

 If I Have an Idea, Do I Need Permission to Try It?

Answer: It depends. Consider weighing the consequences of failure, ensuring that existing important work still gets done, as well as evaluating the time and resource investment and who may be impacted. We also want to, whenever possible, avoid mistakes that are the result of sloppiness. Failure is a possibility with experiments, and that's OK as long as we learn from the failure. When in doubt, your supervisor will be happy to help you decide a path forward.

 How Do I Change My Role in the Organization?

Answer: You should consider both the strengths you would bring to a different role as well as the organizational need. Think about whether the move would fill an important organizational gap and consider the gap you would leave if you were to move. It helps to evaluate who would be affected if you changed roles. Evolving roles may depend on factors like performance and organizational need, but it's a good first step to discuss role changes with your supervisor, director, talent and culture consultant, Human Resources, and/or Organizational Development.

THE UNCERTAINTY CERTAINTY

FAQs are a necessary codification. But understandably, many employees will view their situations as unique. This makes sense; every job, department, and organization chart has its history and nuances. When

Getting the Culture Right

you implement a new culture, all those nuances—all the learned behaviors and previous processes—will not remain in place because, obviously, we are doing something different. But it will be challenging for many employees to adapt. And the only certainty of building a new culture is that people are going to feel what *Leadership on the Line* called "the discomfort of sustained uncertainty."

The penultimate section of the OneCary Toolkit, "Example Scenarios," recognizes that encouraging "every person to raise good ideas and be proactive . . . might mean that employees are faced with situations where there is no precedent on how to proceed." To address various instances of uncertainty, the document outlines scenarios in which "employees may demonstrate the OneCary values and the questions that might be raised in those situations."

Again, I think, it is instructive to share the fruits of our labor.

Navigating Uncertainty

Leadership has asked us to do something for which there is no precedent or established process. Here are some questions to help you formulate a response.

- Is it worth creating a new process or setting a new precedent to fulfill this request?
- Does this request conflict with any established rules or policies?
- Do we comply with this request, or does the situation merit pushback or further conversation?
- Who is invested in this issue?
- What message would the response to this request send to colleagues?
- How can we frame this request and subsequent response to be aligned with our values?
- Does this request conflict with any established rules or policies? Does Cary have legal authority to do this?

The Top of the Arc

You'll notice the guidance here comes in the form of questions, not answers. That's because arriving at the answer to a given situation will arise from discussion, discovery, and analysis. It will come from dialogue. It will come from cocreation. *It will come from OneCary culture.*

The final section of the OneCary Toolkit reiterates how that will happen by advising employees to do two things. First, ask questions: "Talk with your supervisor or talent and culture consultant if you don't understand something." Second, show your support for the initiative by modeling "the behavior and attitudes that you would want to see from others. Stay positive and show confidence that this work is good for us and Cary."

Sounds like unity to me.

CHAPTER 6

MANAGING FOR SUCCESS

I remember that when Sean talked to me in the very beginning, he said changing our culture would take a long time. I nodded and said, "Oh, yeah. Definitely. A couple of years." He said, "No, Renee, like 10 years."

—Renee Poole, chief human resources officer

I learned a long time ago that style is substance. It sends concrete messages—both positive and negative. Therefore, it is a vital part of culture. Let me give you an example.

My first boss had one chair in his office. And that single chair was *the one that he sat on*. I'm not kidding. The first time I walked into his office, I was bewildered. "How come you don't have any chairs in your office?" I asked.

He shot me a look somewhere between contempt and dismissal. "Because the message is get in and get out."

I have to hand it to him: his style was very on point. Message received, right? Here was a guy who didn't want discussion, analysis, or collaboration. He also wanted to show that he didn't care about

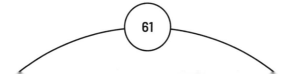

anyone's feelings and had no interest in demonstrating respect for his staff.

How do you think his staff felt about him?

When someone comes into my office to talk, I stand up and suggest we move to a sitting area with a coffee table between us. If I stay seated behind my desk, I'm remaining in a physical position of power. That's not an optimal situation for the substantial, open, frank discussions I want to have with my team or with anyone. So moving to a mutually shared space can change the dynamic.

Say *style* to most people, and it's a safe bet they will think of clothes and fashion. Or they may think of demeanor—how someone conducts themselves. Are they informal or formal? Both these definitions are essential because fashion and demeanor can communicate power, and they have the power to enhance communication. I wear ties nearly every day at work, not just because I have a strong clothes horse gene. The way people dress can send a message. Wearing a great suit and tie (and shoes—don't forget the shoes) projects a serious and conservative demeanor. I need that because it provides cover; the tie offsets my preference for casual, more forthright, honest, and yes, even emotional conversations. If I showed up in jeans and a T-shirt at work, I'd project a style that might indicate I don't care about presentation. But I do.

I care about it because I care about inspiring, motivating, and empowering people in government and about government. But that is harder to do than it should be because too often, the government has an image problem.

I base that statement on 16 percent of Americans telling a well-regarded 2023 survey that they trust the government to do what is right.[1] That poll was focused on the *federal* government. *Local* government has a better reputation in various surveys, which is gratifying. A 2023 Gallup poll reported that 67 percent of respondents trusted local government, while only 32 percent of respondents felt the same toward the legislative branch.[2] Still, that means a huge swath of the nation doesn't trust its leadership. How can we change that? How do we get the best, brightest, most committed workers and the most eager learners to sit with us at the many seats of power?

By acting with style *and* substance. And demonstrating we can get things done.

LOCAL HEROES

I cited the disturbingly low figure of Americans who trust the federal government because I believe people generally think about the national figures who dominate the media when they imagine government. Local government only generates front-page news within its communities, not on a national scale. So local government, traditionally, is not sexy and glamorous, which plays into the image problem. Local government is also not known for lucrative salaries or the kind of bonuses that lure talent to the private sector.

Local government, however, is a compelling platform. Or it should be for many Americans.

Since Calvin Coolidge was misquoted as saying the business of America is business, that idea has taken root as a key part of our national identity. But the education and health industries have the largest number of employees in any American sector.[3] That means many Americans come from community service–oriented backgrounds. Our parents or aunts and uncles were teachers, nurses, lab technicians, members of the military, social workers, union members, clergy, and employees of not-for-profit groups. Arguably, then, we are more a nation of givers than entrepreneurs.

This reality underscores the idea of government of the people, by the people, and for the people. That's why when I hear libertarians and government-shrinking Tea Party figures rail against government, I shudder. What would this country be without government? The highways that connect our cities? Paid for by the government. The GI Bill that sent a generation to college? Paid for by the government. Local schools and libraries? Paid for by the government. The internet? Invented by

The Top of the Arc

the US government's Defense Advanced Research Projects Agency. The massive infrastructure ecosystem of transportation, communications, power, and more that has supported billion-dollar businesses like Amazon, FedEx, Apple, and so many others? Provided and/or regulated by the US government.

Locales that want to create a government that doesn't exist should appeal to both the service-oriented and the career-oriented. Local governments that seek innovation, that want to evolve with the help of new technologies, that seek to grow and create new paradigms and solutions are the ideal platforms and training grounds. In Cary, we don't have quarterly earnings calls driving our decisions. There are no hostile takeover threats. Our work is based on good governance, the direction of the Council, and our culture of informed risk-taking and decision-making that Imagine Cary has mandated.

If, as I've said, people are the building blocks of local government, then good governance dictates getting the right people in the right places. This is why I believed changing culture was going to take time. A local government wants to avoid slashing and burning in the name of progress if that means slashing and burning its own citizens. Good local governance supports communities; it doesn't destroy them.

So the hiring culture in Cary had to evolve. Fortunately, I found the perfect test case when I arrived in Cary to impact that culture.

VULNERABLE IS VALUABLE

One of my first meetings was with Cary's HR director, Renee Poole, who joined the department in 1998 and became its director in 2013. I walked into her office, planning to sit with her for an hour. I had no agenda. Well, that's not completely true. I hoped Renee would be the perfect person to help lead and staff the shift in culture at Cary. If we were going to launch headfirst into the future, we would need a cast of hundreds—or even thousands—who had an open-minded approach to work, to coworkers, to the community, and ultimately, to developing the right skills for the work we needed to be done. That would take equal parts drive, passion, and compassion.

From my point of view, our talk was fantastic. But this is what Renee told my collaborator: "I was glad to have the meeting. I felt very privileged that Sean wanted to meet with me right away. And I remember thinking I could go in there and talk to him in one of two ways. I could have my agenda—boom, boom, boom—and show him all my HR knowledge and knowledge of the organization. Or I could go in and be real and tell him, 'I don't know if I'm the one to lead HR for you.' I had heard Sean give some interviews, and he had a different style, and told my husband, 'I don't know that I'm going to be able to work in that environment.'

"I decided to go down the agenda path until he walked into my office. He was just so easy to talk to and made me feel so at ease that I spit it out. I told him everything—my doubts about adjusting to culture. My concern for the staff. My own skill set compared to what he wanted. And at the end of the meeting, I thought, 'What did I just do?'"

What Renee had done was impress the hell out of me. Here was the woman who had led Cary's staffing—hiring people who ran a smooth, seamless operation that everyone raved about—and she felt vulnerable because of a new boss and the challenge of the unknown. I was convinced she would be able to harness that vulnerability and lead with compassion. She was living with uncertainty. With change. If she could embrace it and adapt, well, that would be ideal. Any town manager who doesn't value the stability that comes with institutional knowledge needs to think again. Of course, I didn't exactly say that, according to Renee: "He said, 'Because you did that—because you have self-doubt. And because you were so vulnerable and honest about that, you are the person to lead the HR initiative here.'"

With the benefit of 20/20 hindsight, I can say my decision was the right one. I encouraged Renee to think bigger when filling open positions. Finding a perfect fit locally was ideal. It would keep the head count low and establish that we were investing in the people who were already part of the team. But I also encouraged her to take her time and be sure we had the right person for each job, a policy that can also keep staffing numbers on the low end. Enlarging our search for candidates was also acceptable, especially for high-priority positions. That meant our job descriptions needed to be more reflective of the culture too. We wanted policymakers with technical and adaptive skills who were OK with risk and who could learn from failure.

"I learned a lot," Renee said. "This idea that these people do their best work when they are challenged and that they become more inspired. Sean pointed out that government systems are designed to insure against failure, so they lock out innovation and risk.

"Another thing I learned from Sean was to think about pace differently. Not everything has to be finite and structured from start to finish. I thought about the pace of what we do. Openings should be filled. But sometimes the right hire is more important than the quick hire.

"'It depends' is a phrase we use all the time, which means it should be dependent on the situation or on the person. If we need a type A to handle a process job because things need to get done, then it's OK to hire that way. But if we hire someone at a supervisor or manager level, we need someone who can be more adaptive. We need candidates who can see things in different ways. Can they pivot? Can they collaborate? Can they fail and learn from that result to get a better outcome on the next project? Do they have space for all that?"

ORGANIZATION CHART INNOVATION AND PACE

Too often, governments operate as rigidly designed systems. There is an organization chart, and the spaces—jobs—in the chart need to be filled. This is a simple, easily understood management device. That said, in some instances, especially with dynamic department leaders and key positions, *designing the org chart around the people* may be more effective. When our staff has a key departure, I tend to reorganize and build a different model to suit the candidate we identify as the right hire. Building a team and creating new spaces in an org chart often produces a better outcome.

Speaking of producing better outcomes, to underscore the flexible, innovative, and initiative-taking leadership I wanted from my senior staff, I actually banished any organization chart for the high-level positions reporting to me. For several years, I refused requests to write one out. I understood the requests. The lack of an org chart made some people uncomfortable. People want to understand chains of command, they want job description clarity, they want territory and responsibility clearly delineated. But local government is like a body; everything is connected. A park isn't just a park, remember? It's an economic development tool. A mixed-use development project isn't just a housing or business complex; it's an anchor for job creation and for a steady tax base. I wanted to encourage my staff to collaborate, and removing the org chart was another way to blow up silos.

When Renee talked about pace, she articulated a management perspective on the ends versus means. Focusing on what will yield the most positive results makes more sense than following ingrained systemic rules about posting and filling a position.

Early in my Cary career, rote government thinking about problem-solving abounded. It was reassuring, in one sense. People felt responsible. They wanted to act. And because they wanted to be team players, they came to me for guidance. "What are we going to do, Sean?" and "What should we do, Sean?" were probably the two most common questions I heard.

My answer? "I don't know what we're going to do."

It's important to note that my response wasn't made solely in regard to hiring decisions. I'd say the same thing when asked about finding money to fund projects. Or when the Town Council asked for my opinion. Not knowing an answer and being comfortable with uncertainty is a positive trait. Too often, saying "I don't know" is taken as an admission of ignorance or weakness or instability. While it can be a sign of those things, to me, it's often a very rational and politically honest statement.

I'm the town manager. I have opinions, but I don't green-light things on a whim. The town votes for a Town Council, which sets agendas, and the town government makes those things happen. As the manager, my responsibility is to ensure our execution is optimized. Very often, that is going to take time. So I'm not stalling when I say "I don't know." Nor am I throwing my hands in the air in a panic.

"I don't know" is an honest response.

So is "*We* need to figure it out."

Maybe I'll switch to that one in the future.

Thankfully, as my efforts to encourage more introspection and outward inquiry have taken root, the question of what we should do has become rarer. The research we do, the information we gather, the data we compile, the creative solutions we generate, the candidates we interview will all gestate with our culture of values and priorities, overseen by the Council and budget realities. Shake it all up, sit with it, look at it, share it. All that is going to tell us what to do next—who to hire, how to train staff or redeploy them, what projects to pursue and what to put on the back burner.

We are now in year 8 of my 10-year prediction to Renee about changing Cary culture. Together with Allison Hutchins's OneCary Toolkit work, we have truly evolved. Staff know they can explore and initiate change. Cary was no stranger to hiring outside consultants in the past. Still, our culture now casts a wider net in search of guidance—consulting with other towns, issuing requests for proposals, working with developers. Sometimes we outsource help nationally to fill senior positions. The HR department has added completely new staff and positions. The org charts are much different too.

A new HR job title emerged: talent and culture consultant. People with this position are members of the HR team assigned to different departments—finance, fire, public works, 311. Their job is to help that department in every way possible. They are encouraged to learn the nuts and bolts of how a department operates, understand its needs, help department leaders with talent management, and talk about how to apply our culture to the work being done.

"Talent and culture consultants are very important," Renee said. "We have these values that everybody can understand. But then how do you take them and apply them to every single type of job, from office work to being out in the field? Seventy-five percent of our workforce is not at town hall. So how do you make these values and culture real for people?"

One way is to treat staff with respect, as codified in our OneCary values. HR has done that in communicating with employees about discussing their roles. Asked how Cary has redeployed and realigned staff, Renee said, "You name a department, and I can give you an example of people who have taken on a new position."

Press her on it, and she might mention that "one of our best talent culture consultants was originally a police officer." This particular officer started his career on patrol and then began working as a school resource officer, which resulted in him working with public schools and principals. He discovered he really enjoyed working with people and discussing policies that improve policing and life in the community. When word got around about the new talent and culture consultant positions, he sought out Renee.

"I had known him for a very long time, and I tried to talk him out of it. I said, 'Do you know what you're giving up as far as police pay later in your retirement benefits?' And he said, 'Yeah, I know. But I love this. I love this work.' So we hired him, and no one has any regrets."

One of the things I love about stories like this, of workers finding their purpose and discovering they can bring their whole selves to work, is that they demonstrate the circularity of good governance in action. By working together, cocreating, and being flexible and open, we take excellent, committed employees and support their quest for more fulfilling work that maximizes their potential. This scenario serves the worker, the team, and therefore, the town. When that happens, Cary's culture takes a giant evolutionary step. We fulfill our endeavor. We go from good to great. Or, even better, from great to awesome.

CHAPTER 7
CONSENSUS BUILDING AND DEVELOPMENT

We had Disney people here, and they wanted to see Downtown Cary Park. They were here for another project. But when they asked to see it, I thought to myself, "When Disney wants to look at your park, well, that's pretty telling."

—Harold Weinbrecht, Cary Mayor and six-term Town Council member

In 2001, long before I set foot in town, the Cary Town Council approved the Town Center Park Concept Plan, which grew out of the Cary Town Center Area Plan that had been approved a year earlier. The Park Concept Plan called for the development in very general terms. Specifics were few and far between. But the park would include an outdoor sculpture, a water feature, and a theater or performance area. A civic and cultural arts report in 2006 also concluded that a performance space should be a requirement. In 2019, Cary citizens approved the "Shaping Cary's Tomorrow Bonds" referendum to spend money on the park. The town procured seven acres of land, but no development work began. When I started as town manager, I heard about the park and learned that the

Consensus Building and Development

Town Council needed a unified vision for the project. Three Council members wanted to use the land as a mixed-use economic development project, while four members favored building a park. Obviously, 4–3 constitutes a majority. However, as town manager, I was leery of embarking on an enormous project—especially one requiring the town to approve a sizable bond—without unqualified support. There is always an element of risk in any undertaking. I wanted my bosses to be unified and excited, not ambivalent and divided.

After listening to the Council members' points and counterpoints, one almost comical irony quickly became clear. As far as the park was concerned, neither side could see the forest for the trees; they were fighting for no reason.

I told the Council I had good news for them: "It can be both a park *and* an economic development project. If you build a park—not just a 'normal' neighborhood park, but something truly unique that looks and feels like nothing else in North Carolina—you'll get all the economic development you want, and you will have a world-class park."

I didn't know precisely what a unique park would entail. I just knew that if it were special, if it became a lure with uniquely stylized buildings, elaborate landscaping, space for performances, or a world-class playground—and ideally, all those things and more—the domino effect of development would follow. This is not particularly original thinking on my part. If you build it, the mutated quote from *Field of Dreams* goes, they will come. (The line in the movie is "*He* will come.") And that makes sense. Developers like to build stores, restaurants, and residential buildings around anchor destinations. Think about Central Park in New York—the luxurious apartments and museums of Fifth Avenue and Central Park West went up *after* the city designated a mind-blowing 840 acres to be transformed for public use. Think about any unique urban jewel where people like to gather—Miami Beach, Old Pasadena. Money follows money. I shared these observations with the Council, and suddenly the faction that wanted to build multiuse economic development projects agreed that a park might not be such a bad idea after all. Everyone was on board. But now the hard part:

We still needed a world-class park.

The Top of the Arc

The 20 years of discussion and kicking the can down the road had to end. We held the first big meeting to finally, really, seriously embark on the park, and the turnout was huge.

Many, if not all, of the Parks and Recreation staff were there. At some point, someone took the floor and said, "OK, Sean, we're going to need $10 million for this park." People started listing park features, such as playgrounds and a sports field. I listened for a bit and realized that, similar to the previously divided Council, the staff hadn't fully grasped the opportunities our future park might afford us. I wanted everyone to recalibrate. "We're not going to do that," I said. "The first thing we're going to do is set the budget at $50 million."

This immediately got everyone's attention.

It was a large number.

I continued, "Not only that, but we're going to pay $10,000 or $20,000 for three or four of the best architects in the nation to come and bid on building this thing."

No doubt, people in the room wondered if I was serious or crazy.

I might have been crazy, but I was definitely serious. People began to grasp the vision. They began to get excited. I wondered if there would be a backlash. Would the group of naysayers who surfaced to protest Imagine Cary reappear? But people wanted to hear more.

I explained my plan for paying landscape architects for their proposals. As with all big projects, we needed to issue an RFP—a request for proposal. In my experience, one of the problems with RFPs is that submitting innovative, bid-winning plans costs firms money. They devote time and staffing to come up with ideas. But what business wants to invest in something that may not yield a return? To ensure we got the best efforts and to show our future partners we were serious, my idea was to let bidders know we would award the three or four finalists $10,000 each to fund their final proposals. The plan was to incentivize the most talented firms in the world to deliver their best work.

Then we would have to do our best work and evaluate what Cary wanted.

CONSENSUS 101

To me, the most hurtful thing you can do to someone is not invite them to a party.

This is not an overstatement. Inclusion is important. Participation, or the invitation to participate, is the foundation of government. Yet it can feel like a rarity. And when it does happen, participation can be heated and divisive. Too often, then, governing conjures up images of anger-filled community board meetings, "Not in My Backyard" placards, and dramatic gestures to embarrass or quiet a member of the opposition—even though they are fellow citizens.

Sowing the seeds of good governance with fair and open dialogue and honest listening is a way of being respectful. Respect can pay huge dividends.

I'm going to make a point about those dividends, but I want to be clear: Respect is not a tool that I wield to manipulate people. It is a best practice for living life, for feeling better about yourself and helping others feel good.

I aspire to live this way. Inclusion, this idea about working with elected officials, came from a genuine belief that people should never feel excluded in problem-solving. I had three best men at my wedding because I wasn't going to pick just one.

People matter.

This is not woo-woo, kumbaya mumbo-jumbo. This is how I want to live.

When making decisions about Downtown Cary Park, I sought the input far and wide, but certainly, I wanted the Council involved. On a fundamental level, as the people's elected servants—not to mention my bosses—they deserved that respect. They had approved the expenditures too. So in many ways, their reputations were on the line. But on a practical level, we consulted them as a demonstration of respect and trust, which engendered their respect and trust. All the cards—I mean, designs—were on the table. Nothing was hidden.

The Top of the Arc

Returning to the dividends of respect, in most situations, *the more you invite people in, the less they will intrude.* This is a counterintuitive idea. Most people will want to avoid getting into the nitty-gritty when dealing with complex problems that require rigorous training in specific fields, such as architecture, engineering, public utilities, materials, and construction. That said, long-serving town councils generally have experience with high-level project management. That's what they do: set policy and help oversee its execution. By including the Council in the design review process, we got some excellent perspectives while earning their trust and support.

UPSOURCING

In 2019, Cary citizens approved a $200-plus-million general obligation bond measure—with $50 million of it to support the park. Examining the responses to our request for proposals, the town selected the park design from the Boston location of OJB Landscape Architecture, an award-winning landscape and urban planning practice. OJB's Cody Klein brought in Jeffry Burchard, winner of the 2020 American Institute of Architecture's Young Architects Award and partner at the design powerhouse Machado Silvetti, to develop and orchestrate the larger structures of Downtown Cary Park.

More than 2,000 people worked on shaping and building the park. For Burchard, though, the most important aspect of collaboration may have been the invisible throughline between Cary's approach to the project and the mission of both architectural partners: "We share a common belief that we don't leave vision to somebody else. We're able to absorb and learn from and build upon and make better. But there's nobody else responsible for the vision and responsible for the implementation. And there's a degree of risk that comes with that kind of approach."

Burchard also told a friend, "Give the Town of Cary everything they want—that's Sean's vision. And that translates into enthusiasm for the residents, it translates into the town being involved and engaged. Sean never said, 'Make a round building.' Sean said, 'Make great architecture.' He never said, 'Make a park that has all these wandering paths with fire pits in the middle of them and all these different level changes and . . . giant birds to climb on in a playground.' They never dictated those things. They gave us access to the resources so that we would get inspired by them and then bring the design along."

Those resources? I'd argue that the biggest one was the Town of Cary itself. Because, Cary being Cary, we told the experts to find out what we wanted.

"It was great," Burchard told my collaborator. "In master planning, we had workshops and public meetings that OJB organized. Hundreds of community members came out and engaged in active workshops, telling us what they wanted to be able to do in their park. This was another really interesting thing about Sean and maybe about the town—I don't know if it's a thing they practice all the time—but at the beginning, we talked about intangible qualities rather than specific things. In landscape architecture, that means 'I want to be able to bring my dog there, I want to be able to play chess there, I want to be able to eat lunch there, I want to listen to a concert there.' But we didn't talk about 'OK, what *kind* of dog park do you want? What *kind* of playground? Or what *kind* of performance pavilion do you want?'

"As designers, the intangibles help us catch more about people's interests. You can gauge what people are talking about, activities or experiences, and things that can appeal to a broader group of people. That's more useful than someone saying, 'Here's a historic building, or here's a building that looks like a contemporary building—which one do you like?'"

These kinds of exchanges—I'm tempted to call them "intangibles-finding missions"—were a key element to the discovery process. This was not surprising given the town's success in gathering feedback for Imagine Cary. The workshops and meetings provided additional inspiration and new frames of reference for Burchard and his team. But they were never presented as strict guidelines. And I'm glad that we left it to the experts.

The experts, per Burchard, were glad too.

"This is going to sound really self-serving, but the town let us lead the design process. And I think that matters," Burchard said. "We were not hired to deliver a project that had already been decided. They could have very well said, 'We already know what this project is. We know what the components are. We know what we want it to look like. City council members have gone and seen buildings they like, and here they are.' They could have done this, but despite all of their vision and their confidence and their money, they still understood that they didn't know how to get the best version of what they were after."

I was amazed by what the proposals helped us learn. We were after something new, something different, something that connected us to the land and the town, yet something that would take visitors on a journey to a new environment they had never experienced before, complete with new horizons.

The designs OJB and Machado Silvetti came up with had plenty of new environments. Walking through the park, visitors would encounter pavilions built at different levels, curving pathways, elevated walkways, and bubbling-brook waterways that fed an environmentally functional water feature that would serve as a drainage conduit for the downtown area. These features created new, evolving vistas as visitors traversed the park. Adding elements of surprise were singular wood-and-glass buildings with circular designs. "Our buildings, which are round and curvilinear, don't look like anything else in pure Cary," Burchard admitted.

He was right. These architectural elements were a significant stylistic departure for Cary. I loved them. To me, an urban park meant building new, singular structures. Otherwise, what was the point? But Cary being Cary, the new look flew in the face of established building codes, so both the town and the architect needed to adapt.

"Our buildings didn't fit exactly with the traditional model design standards," said Burchard. "So we did a little bit of adjustment and worked with Cary's Planning and Development Services. If people don't see things as black and white, if there's room for conversation in the pursuit of something great, then you can collaborate. There's a lot of

Consensus Building and Development

room in Cary. We knew we had the enthusiasm and the vision of the town manager and of the Parks and Rec staff."

There's another term for that enthusiasm: political will. The town had approved the expenditure for the park, the Council had approved the planners. Obviously, rules needed to be followed. But just as obviously, there had to be room for discussion because political will existed to get the park done.

In the end, the reviews turned into a hybrid of barter and architectural analysis sessions. The planners found a masonry bond similar to bonds used in previous municipal buildings. Walls, fences, and porches found on Academy Street echoed similar elements of the master plan. Bit by bit, with changes here and there or tweaks to materials or design, our collaboration led to creation.

THEY WILL COME

With Downtown Cary Park underway, developers began to focus on projects within neighboring blocks of the seven-acre site. Some, like a proposal for a mixed-use complex called The Walker, demonstrated an instant understanding of Cary's vision for a more urban environment. Located at the southern edge of the park, The Walker, which was approved in 2020, offers 125 luxury apartments, about 16,000 square feet of ground-floor retail space, and a future building designated for office and retail use, all built around a parking garage. By 2024, it had an occupancy rate of 95 percent and an award-winning restaurant.

That's just one success story. Interest in the area has soared since the park was announced, as has property valuation in single-family houses. Chatham Street, which is perpendicular to Academy Street, the main thoroughfare to the park, has a development underway. A second parking garage is also under construction. And the town is weighing a sizable redesign of its transit center, which has resulted in 18 applications from many of North Carolina's leading developers.

The Top of the Arc

Downtown Cary Park opened on Sunday, November 19, with a ribbon-cutting ceremony. A whopping 35,000 people showed up for the first weekend of festivities. "You can expect to wander into wonder," said Joy Ennis, the park's general manager, on the opening day. She was right. The park received rave reviews from the general public; travel- and community-focused sites like Tripadvisor and Yelp are filled with positive feedback and four-star ratings. The response in the media has been gratifying as well. The long-running *Architect's Newspaper* wrote that the park "redefines the town" and saluted the design for "ample amounts of open green space as well as programmed areas based on historic, cultural, and environmental needs." Reading the paper's detailed appraisal provides a sweeping experiential analysis of the elements of the park that I, as a nonarchitect, would be hard-pressed to come up with. Here's a favorite passage:

> Throughout the park, shade gardens, perennial gardens, wetland and aquatic plantings, pollinator gardens, and native meadows abound underneath generous tree canopies. The square is centered by Academy Plaza and Pavilion which features a vast stormwater pond that helps collect and detain rainwater across the park. . . .
>
> Visitors can elect to meander through the paved walkways or take the long route on an elevated path that zigzags through the site. Metal railings and a sculptural, nest-like piece are installed along the elevated walk.
>
> On a separate corner of the park, The Gathering House & Gardens provides seamless indoor-outdoor spaces that offer intimate areas for community, family, and corporate gatherings. Close by is The Bark Bar, an open-air beverage pavilion-slash-restaurant to the park's eastern edge. Here, an S-shaped structure gives people access to active and social recreation areas.[1]

The article also highlights many other aspects of the park, including the two other pavilions, the Great Lawn and its amphitheater, and the

Consensus Building and Development

Nest, the park's play area that features two towering wooden cardinals, our state bird, that are visual magnets for adults and must-climb-and-explore structures for kids, with multiple points of entry and, in the case of a long metal tube slide, exit.

Of course, there is so much more: 36 varieties of trees native to North Carolina, over 60,000 plants, amazing public art installations that range from incorporating Cary's history to modern light sculptures, a dog park, a gentle waterfall.

In other words, it is a bountiful park. I won't say there's something for everyone; I'm sure someone was dreaming of a merry-go-round, for instance. But there is a lot to like, or should I say, love. For me, the spiraling designs that swirl everywhere—not just the curving pathways or the circular bar and the swelling, eye-catching amphitheater on the Great Lawn—really feel unique. They remind me of the geometric designs kids make with Spirograph kits come to life.

THE ARC AND THE PARK

One of my favorite small touches is an informational plaque posted in the park that speaks to the cresting motifs that abound. It talks about the park design as an inspiring metaphor for the town itself:

> An integral design element of the Downtown Cary Park, arcs serve as a personal reminder to those who created this inspirational place—and a message to every person who visits—that it is up to each of us to keep Cary "at the top of the arc." Parks, people, even entire communities evolve, and we—all of us—shoulder the incredible responsibility for creating and recreating the best Cary possible—for keeping Cary "Cary." Cary's setbacks are our setbacks, and Cary's successes are our successes.

No doubt there may be cynics out there who view this as civic-minded propaganda. I view it as the truth, a reminder that we all share

The Top of the Arc

responsibility for creating our own realities and our own communities. If citizens don't take ownership, who will?

So as the plaque implies, the park itself represents the top of the Cary arc—a metaphor I find both powerfully inspiring and challenging. Aiming for excellence and then achieving that goal requires dreaming and analyzing, investing and taking risks, and embracing responsibility. Repeating that process requires building a culture that embodies and sustains our commitment to excellence, to staying at the top of the arc.

The response has been beyond gratifying. The park serves as a lure for the entire Triangle region in general and a conduit to all kinds of commerce and culture. The Cary Library abuts the park on its south end. If visitors cross the street, they arrive at the Cary Arts Center, which hosts a 431-seat theater and a slew of classes in painting, drawing, acting, dance, pottery, sewing, jewelry making, and more. The neighborhood also boasts restaurants, a hotel, a microbrewery with a beer garden, and shops. The mixed-use economic development project that Cary's Town Council coveted now exists. The entire downtown will continue to evolve in new and dynamic ways. I expect many things will change. New arcs will appear on the horizon. And that is just the way it should be.

CHAPTER 8
CHANGING THE HORIZONS

FENTON AND SOUTH HILLS

Plan: n. A design, a proposal.
   An organized (and usually detailed) proposal according to which something is to be done; a scheme of action; a strategy; a programme, schedule. Also in a weakened sense: a method or way of proceeding; an intention or ambition for the future (usually in *plural*).
—*Oxford English Dictionary*

Ambiguity: n.
   Originally and chiefly with reference to language: the fact or quality of having different possible meanings; capacity for being interpreted in more than one way; (also) lack of specificity or exactness.
—*Oxford English Dictionary*

A curious thing about plans—especially government plans—is that when we write them, print them, and read them, they are two-dimensional and often feel finite. They exist on paper or as computer files. By definition,

The Top of the Arc

they specify what "is to be done," essentially codifying the design, the action, and the process. But some plans, like the Imagine Cary Community Plan, leave room for ambiguity.

Now, don't get me wrong. I love a blueprint with precise details, numbers, and schematics as much as the next project manager. But Cary was very lucky to leave room for ambiguity. If Imagine Cary—the very name suggests a level of improvisation and creativity—had over-planned, it's likely the town would be twisted in knots with addendums, codicils, hearings, hearings about hearings, and lawsuits. I understand that those kinds of messy outcomes are part of the democratic process. But when a plan leads to paralysis, who suffers? The town and its citizens. In this instance, the local government would have failed them.

The Imagine Cary Community Plan contained specifics. *General* specifics. It named several "destination centers" designated as "mixed use centers that include an integrated mix of commercial (shopping, services), office, and residential uses, arranged in a walkable pattern with an active pedestrian realm where buildings front streets."[1] These centers, the plan said, might be designed for special uses. One of those areas was the Eastern Cary Gateway, an 800-acre Special Planning Area, one-third of which was undeveloped. Within that gateway footprint were two established destinations. The first, WakeMed Soccer Park, was the town-owned-and-operated 150-acre sporting complex, comprising a 10,000-seat soccer stadium and seven fields. It drew more than 200,000 visitors annually. The second, Triangle Aquatic Center, was the number-one venue for aquatic events in the state, serving nearly half a million visitors. The area also bordered Raleigh, which, as the state capital and the home to North Carolina State University and its 37,000 students, made it an ideal conduit to a population of about half a million people. So the architects of Imagine Cary were quite savvy; from a purely geographic point of view, this was land use that, with the right initiatives, improved the quality of life in the town, lured more visitors, and boosted the economy.

Changing the Horizons

As it happened, a 92-acre parcel of undeveloped land in the Eastern Cary Gateway was owned by the state of North Carolina, and the Columbia Development Group had obtained the right to purchase that land. This was fine per Imagine Cary, which envisioned a mixed-use center to stoke employment that would improve future transit and pedestrian connectivity—via roads, a greenway, and municipal transport—within the corridor and also help revitalize Cary Towne Center, a 1979 mall that was once anchored by Dillard's, Macy's, JCPenney, and Sears. The Towne Center had been hit by hard times, but increasing traffic to the area would foster new development. And a new build-out would provide a throughline of activity all the way to Downtown Cary.

In 2016, the Columbia Development Group submitted a plan for the 92 acres that was very in line with old Cary: low-density suburban housing, strip or single-use business structures to be anchored by a grocery store, and surface parking. In terms of the vision that was shaped in the work-in-progress Imagine Cary plan, this was not what the town wanted. The proposal was rejected.

Russ Overton, our deputy town manager and COO who has been instrumental in development planning, recalled, "One of the Council members, I think it was Jennifer Robinson, said, 'I don't want this kind of low density; I really want to wait for great.' And she was right."

Columbia was not happy with the town and went back to the drawing board to work on rezoning plans. State officials who had sold the property to Columbia weren't particularly pleased either, according to Russ. There was some concern that officials might punish Cary and approve a small institutional development—in the form, perhaps, of a small state office building—and cut the town out of having any say or including the resulting project in the town's tax base. That fear motivated Cary's team of planners and business developers to get serious about articulating what the town considered "great" in a manner that would sync up with the Imagine Cary document.

As Russ recalled, "Of course, that pissed the developers off, because they're ready to move fast, and nothing really happens fast in Cary. It happens methodically. Fast, generally speaking, is never well done. So it was very contentious. In their minds, we delayed things for two years. And in our minds, we were going fast for two years. But we adopted an Eastern Cary Gateway plan that was, technically, like a month ahead of the rest of the Imagine Cary plan. But I think the Eastern Cary Gateway really clicked with Columbia's invitation to go down and see a multiuse development outside of Atlanta.

"Sean insisted we visit. He said, 'Well, you got to go look at it.' So we saw a mixed-use development that was unlike anything we have in Cary. And it was probably a spark that ignited the project to really move forward."

The Town Council and staff visited Avalon, an 86-acre development in Alpharetta, Georgia. It includes blocks of retail, residential housing, restaurants, office space, fountains, a movie theater, and a hotel with a conference center. It is a pedestrian-friendly zone within a more classically suburban environment.

"It gelled for them," Jamie Schwedler, a Raleigh real estate lawyer who was instrumental in addressing zoning issues for many Cary projects, recalled. "They saw the possibility and said, 'This is what we could have. This is the kind of amenity that could be brought to Cary.' The town really didn't have a mixed-use development of that scale at the time. It was going to be not an employment center but really a high-end, mixed-use, retail-rich environment with a kind of curated experience, which they didn't really have a template for."

Now a template, a much more detailed template, began to emerge. Infrastructure requirements were collected. The developers and the town began discussing how to fortify the land to prevent erosion. Building retaining walls and stormwater detention vaults would require power and sewage lines, which meant working to expand access to utilities. That required critical back-end planning, the necessities people so often take for granted and don't relish debating.

Conversely, the front end of development—what it looks like, how it will function, and what the user experience will be—is something everyone cares about. That's what people are invested in: the total environment. To provide clarity and avoid logjams, town departments and the

Council worked with Columbia to arrive at a set of new rules specifically for a new development called Fenton. A more urban landscape with new storefronts demanded new signage rules. The town couldn't expect a retailer or restaurant chain to invest in leasing thousands of square feet for the modest signage allowances in the older Cary neighborhoods. Similarly, future tenants of the million square feet of office space in Fenton would require additional adaptive measures. Streetscapes would be different, requiring new lighting. To avoid cookie-cutter buildings, we needed new regulations for differing elevations.

In April 2017, Columbia submitted a *Community Design Guidebook*. For our internal development team, this was a game changer.

"It was the quality of it," Russ explained. "They created a design guidebook that committed to standards that surpassed design standards that we have. It also included pictures of what the properties looked like. So it created its own standards and rezoning standards. It was a first of its kind, and we've reused it on other rezoning projects to simplify the process to show people a vision of what's coming."

Now the town and the developers had a document—a plan—that gave the Council something semitangible to review. And it gave Columbia and Cary's development teams an opportunity to expand on their plans and answer questions.

"What's unique about Cary's Council is its willingness to be open to be educated," said Schwedler. "This was so different from what the town had seen in the past. But after doing their due diligence, they were able to say, 'These are things we like' [and] 'These are things we don't like,' and [they] brought together that project."

It also allowed us to develop a common language and submit an amended rezoning application. In November 2018, Cary and Columbia signed an agreement establishing the creation of a mixed-use development on those 92 acres.

The Eastern Cary Gateway "destination center" finally had a name, courtesy of the Columbia Design Group. The development would be called Fenton as a nod to the town's namesake, Samuel Fenton Cary, an Ohio congressman and temperance leader much admired by town founder Frank Page.

Having designed Fenton, Columbia brought in a development partner to help seal and deliver it. Hines, one of the leading real estate developers in the US, joined the project, and Paul Zarian, the director for Hines's Raleigh office, took the reins. Zarian was on somewhat familiar territory—he had moved to Cary.

"Fenton was unlike anything that not only Cary had done but many municipalities throughout the country could have done," Zarian recalled. "This was the first development agreement where there was a public contribution to off-site infrastructure. Without that, the project would not have started. It was an absolutely necessary part of the process."

Zarian was alluding to certain requirements in the Imagine Cary plan that envisioned the construction of public facilities—roads and greenways—that were vital to the project, not just for connecting traffic to Fenton, but for connecting the Eastern Cary Gateway to itself so that visitors to Fenton could make their way to the WakeMed Soccer Park or the aquatic center by bike, foot, or car without going miles out of their way. The town agreed to reimburse developers for the build-out costs for these enhancements.

For Zarian, that level of compromise was part of the process: "Cary had a very open mind as they approached coming up with a new process for approving architecture and signage. Throughout the town, there's a fairly strict code that governs those aspects. But for Fenton, they purposely wanted and intentionally wanted something that was different. They worked with the development team to create a mechanism to provide that flexibility, which they knew would give them . . . the more organic project that they wanted but also allowed them to have a certain level of insight in terms of what would ultimately be delivered there. So it required a complete change in mindset versus the status quo."

Powered by the new mindset—which I like to think of as *creative collaboration*—the ambiguous plan morphed into an actionable one. Phase 1, approved in 2020, included nearly 200,000 square feet of office space, 368,000 square feet of commercial space, and 400,000 square feet dedicated to 357 dwelling units. Additionally, the details codified street layout, utility infrastructure, building locations, architecture, hardscape, and landscaping. The site opened in June 2022, and eight months later, 92 percent of the retail space was rented to the likes of Sephora, Warby Parker, Bluemercury, Pottery Barn, Madewell, and Sports & Social, which at 22,000 square feet is the largest sports bar in the Triangle. In early 2023, residents began moving into available rental units, and 50 percent of the office retail space was leased. Given the glut of post-COVID office space at the time, finding new tenants to fill 100,000 square feet of office space might seem like a remarkable achievement. But I take it as confirmation that the town got Fenton—our new "destination center"—right. What business wouldn't want to provide quality-of-life improvements to its employees, from ample parking to multiple food, shopping, and entertainment choices; to local housing options; to world-class sporting facilities? And all within walking distance. Additionally, having multiple businesses in one centralized environment increases the pool of prospective employees and new job openings. So theoretically, both employers and staff are in win-win positions. You often hear about Silicon Valley start-ups offering staffers food perks or a gaming room at the office. Fenton offers the makings of an urban environment, a minicity that, in the future, will grow wider and more vertical.

SOUTH HILLS

The South Hills shopping center, just off Interstate 440 and the interchange to I-40 and US 1, was Cary's first mall. When developer David Martin finished the initial site in 1965, the redbrick strip mall was anchored by a grocery store and housed about 25 smaller shops.[2] The build-out continued, as Martin developed 370,000 square feet of shopping center and retail use, sprawling outdoor parking, and Cary's first large motel. In America, the evolution of retail space has shifted radically in the last 50 years, from mom-and-pop localized businesses, to

The Top of the Arc

strip malls, to indoor malls, to big-box stores, and most recently, to the Main Street– and mall-busting shop-anywhere competition of cyberspace. But the Martin family held on until 2021.

"This group of developers bought it, and their vision for this, now, is basically streets of Philadelphia. Not the Bruce Springsteen song but the fact that it will have small blocks—so emphasizing form over use—to create, really, a walkable environment with vertically mixed structures," recalled Scot Berry, Cary's chief development officer and assistant town manager. "Sean opened the vision. He always says, 'Don't put restraints on your thinking.' So the developer comes in and hears that, and then they hire this great land-use planner. And he hears that and gets super excited as well. When that happens, you come up with this vision from a group that, really, was just going to buy the mall and repurpose the space. But now they say, 'We're going to buy the mall, and now we have a 25-year plan to create, basically, another city.'"

I am guilty as charged. But remember, cocreation is a two-way street. It feeds off collaboration. When Scot tells me about developers and the projects they've done and the plans they are considering, that gets me excited too. When I thought about South Hills, with its fantastic access to the rest of the Triangle, it got me thinking about what the Cary community needed. How would it benefit our citizens? And how might it benefit others in the Research Triangle? What could we create that would make it, like Fenton or Downtown Cary Park, a "destination-location," to use the phrase in the Imagine Cary Community Plan?

I started kicking around ideas. One thing I wanted to do was build a 21st-century community center for the town. We had world-class soccer, tennis, and water sports facilities. But I wanted something that would specifically benefit Cary's general population, especially for people who might be allergic to soccer, tennis, or lap pools. Since our three community centers were fairly ancient, I thought a state-of-the-art recreation center for indoor sports activities would be a great new asset for the town.

"We pitched it to the developers," Scot Berry recalled. "A rec center with a gym big enough to fit 16 basketball courts. And it became what they wanted to do. They saw us as ready to put public money into something because that is one way to create an initial tax base. But they also saw that it creates a halo effect. Usually, developers are not crazy about changing plans. But quickly realizing this development had grown, they said, 'Maybe we need to get rid of these little condos and build something with more calories.'"

Those calories would now include just what you might expect an urban hub to have—not just a stand-alone attraction but a hotel, office space, retail space, and new roads.

URBAN DESIGN UNITY

The development group spearheading the project, now called NP South Hills LLC, had amassed over 44 acres of land. There was a general vision—small city blocks surrounding a 4,000-seat arena and rec center. But now it was time to move from blue-sky planning to blueprint reality. For South Hills, the developers hired David Green, master planning urban design leader and principal at Arup, one of the leading sustainability design firms in the world. His track record was exemplary, and we were excited to see our vision collide with his expertise to produce, if not fireworks, then plans that would dazzle and delight with unexpected form and function.

David's arrival coincided with the recent opening of the Cary Urban Design Studio overseen by our new urban design manager, Allen Davis. Cary owns a two-story building next to the Cary Theater on Chatham Street in the downtown area. The first floor has a coffee shop; the third floor has lots of windows, a balcony, and great light. When the tenant left, we renovated the space, and the urban design studio was born. A place *near* town hall but not *in* town hall. The distance, like the office itself, was intended to create a safe space to discuss urban planning. It's not a high-tech wonderland with advanced 3D digital modeling workstations. Of course there are computer screens, but the big win was lots of open space with tables and chairs—places to cocreate and build on the recent successes.

"Fenton was a very successful project for Cary. But we, in this project, we're trying to push beyond that," Green said, stressing that the arena and recreation center were going to be huge draws both locally and regionally. And that required "managing the parking and understanding exactly what needs to happen." He continued, "And so [Cary was] very open to a lot of these ideas. And the goal in all of this was that the town would actually take what we're doing in this core area and expand it, creating a planning district in this area that Cary can build on."

That future, as Green advocated, involves 20,000 square feet of public outdoor space in South Hills, pedestrian walkways, bicycle and scooter parking for two-wheeled commuters, and structured parking decks at the outskirts of the development to foster a more pedestrian-friendly experience. The rezoning proposal submitted to the town calls for 935,000 square feet of office space, 235,000 square feet of research lab space, 550,000 square feet of retail space, and 350 hotel rooms. The area's future also involves eventually recasting the older multifamily housing stock just north of South Hills. "It will get redeveloped with smaller blocks—a lot of pedestrian-oriented streets that then connect all the way up," Green explained. "And at some point, you're going to connect all this up, and you'll be able to walk in about 20 minutes from South Hills to Fenton, which will be pretty cool."

Green and others began articulating these ideas while meeting with Cary officials. He even commented, unbidden, about the process and the place.

"There was almost complete alignment," Green said, offering shout-outs to a host of town departments. "But one of the interesting things that brought us all together was a very high-functioning urban design studio. We were able to use that as a center where all of these different constituents could come together in almost a neutral setting and really talk through, in an interesting way, opportunities for the project.

"The town was very open to us presenting some, I wouldn't say radical, but certainly unconventional ideas about the way this would get developed. Normally, we would have been pushing up against challenges with the town, overcoming regulatory issues, overcoming traffic issues, overcoming broader development issues, but with Cary, it was never like that. They grabbed onto the vision from the very beginning. They said, 'This is what we're really looking for,' which happened to align with some more broad, set visions coming from the Mayor and the Council, which was fantastic."

ADAPTIVE ENGAGEMENT

As the South Hills project evolved, so did plans to add a new community center in western Cary and continue to build out Cary's greenways and parks. The Town Council voted to present Cary citizens with a referendum on a $560 million parks and recreation bond. As with previous bonds, the Council grouped these projects together as a package deal with specific earmarks. Sixty million dollars would go toward a tennis park expansion. Twenty million dollars would fund master plans for an Asian garden and nature park. Thirty million dollars would fund the 2018 Adaptive Stormwater initiative, a three-mile greenway linking Downtown Cary Park, Fenton, WakeMed Soccer Park, the Triangle Aquatic Center, and South Hills District. A multipurpose community center in western Cary required $150 million to fund. The largest project was the South Hills recreation center development, which was budgeted for $300 million.

The Town Council also brought a second referendum to raise $30 million on an affordable housing plan. Together, we were asking voters to do two things: (1) approve spending over half a billion dollars for community enhancements and (2) pay off this debt with a property tax rate increase of nine cents that would be implemented in separate three-cent increases from 2026 to 2030.

To state the obvious, $590 million was a lot of money to borrow. From my perspective, Cary would be investing in projects that replicated both Downtown Cary Park and Fenton. Remember? A park or state-of-the-art community center could also be viewed as mixed-use economic development projects. These new initiatives would create value and opportunity. But this narrative of the future collided with another reality.

Let me explain.

In summer 2024, before the referendum vote occurred, Cary's Town Council did something it had never done in recent history. It raised the town's property tax rate by eight cents—a hike that still left Cary with the lowest property tax rate of any municipality in the county. The real estate market in Cary, like in many parts of the US, had been booming. The assessments determined by Wake County reflected residential property values in Cary increasing an average of 57 percent and commercial properties 39 percent since the previous appraisals.

For property owners in Cary, these soaring valuations were good news, ostensibly delivering huge returns on investment. But those returns didn't occur in a vacuum. Along with both Cary's and the county's property tax rate increases that were applied to those new, higher values, prices were rising all over the country as the national inflation numbers climbed, which of course had real administration costs for the town. The economic challenges meant making some difficult choices as the Council focused largely on maintaining quality services. "We're doing everything we can without cutting services to keep costs as low as possible, which is obviously very challenging in a high-inflation environment," I told local reporters.

I echoed the sentiments of my bosses. Council Member Jennifer Robinson told the *News & Observer* that the budget deliberations were the hardest in years. "We're not raising taxes flippantly," Robinson said. "We have always said that we would only raise taxes if we absolutely needed to. The inflation that we're experiencing is impacting us at home, it's impacting this organization in the same manner. Everything costs more."[3]

No doubt the tax increase was painful for some, especially for residents who live on a fixed income. However, the Council determined it was necessary. And given the surge in valuations, eight cents didn't

Changing the Horizons

seem to be *that* much. As I mentioned, even with the increase, Cary property tax rates remained the lowest in Wake County.

On November 5, 2024, Cary voters rejected both referendums. Up to 44,109 people voted for the parks and recreation bond, but 54,114 voted against it. The vote on the affordable housing bond was even closer, voted down 50,402 to 47,576.[4] A postelection town survey of voters told us the reason: the majority of voters, still processing the recent 2024 tax increase, did not want another one to support these initiatives.

It's easy to view referendums in up-or-down victories or defeats. But none of the referendum projects, which were inspired by the Imagine Cary Community Plan, have been completely wiped off the table forever. Only the proposed specific funding mechanism that would have propelled the projects forward was stopped.

The Town Council has been recalibrating, processing the message of the voters we serve, and putting our adaptive leadership skills to the test. The Cary Town Council must figure out new ways to create affordable initiatives. We will continue to look for new cost-saving innovations, creative budgets, win-win partnerships, and untapped revenue sources. We must invest in our people to hit new highs of cocreation. I am just riffing here, but perhaps the greenway extension can find additional funding via the utilities budget. Maybe we'll find new ways to lower operational expenses in various services. Maybe Nike will want to underwrite the tennis center expansion or new partners will surface to fund the Asian garden.

As for the South Hills project, the developers now have a seven-acre parcel of land, the site earmarked for the community center, that will need to be rethought and developed. What does the future hold for that land? The mind wanders: a world-class museum, a futuristic 21st-century amusement park, a theater complex—who knows? But eventually, a development agreement with details about what the town will contribute for road and water infrastructure—which is what we did with Fenton—will be signed, and Cary will continue to adapt and grow.

To be clear, the cocreation of South Hills isn't just the Council's vision or me pulling strings. The town gave its tacit approval back when the Imagine Cary Community Plan passed unanimously.

The Top of the Arc

In case anyone thinks that plan isn't a foundational document, well, perhaps they can hear praise for its foresight in something David Green said in an interview: "My view of the Town of Cary has changed 180 degrees. I never thought it was bad. I just thought it was well run and nice, but also a conventional, suburban town that was associated with a larger city. And I've come to understand since then that that's entirely untrue. Knowing a bit about the history now and working with them a great deal over the last year, I've come to realize that they're incredibly progressive, and the project that we're doing is one of the most progressive redevelopment projects like this in the country.

"I've worked with many different government entities over the last 30 years. But I can honestly say that Cary has been—and I'm talking both globally and nationally—the best, most collaborative group of city town officials I've ever worked with. And that's really hard to believe because you wouldn't think, if you're throwing a dart at the world, that the most progressive, collaborative people that you work with are in a kind of suburban community in the Research Triangle area."

CHAPTER 9

HOW TO BE A GOOD TOWN MANAGER

I didn't know if I wanted to be a manager before working with Sean. And now I know: I don't want to be a manager. I know that because I could never commit the personal sacrifice Sean commits to his job, especially with Council members. He listens to them when they call at night or whenever. And he never stops listening to them. He's always there for them. He's always going to try and find a win for them.

—Allison Hutchins, director of learning and organizational development

Every town manager should have opinions and vision—and so should every police officer, every solid waste worker, and every 311 citizen advocate. That's part of living. During the active parts of our day, we all observe, dream, and analyze, and certain ideas or feelings begin to take hold and become more prominent and worthy of being shared. But it is not every town manager's job to push their personal opinions or implement their vision.

That's because when it comes to governance, everyone's opinions and vision matter, but there is one select group of people whose opinions

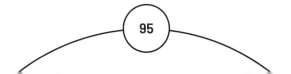

The Top of the Arc

and vision matter more than everyone else's. That group would be the Town Council (a.k.a. the town manager's bosses). This is the group of elected officials who have been entrusted to lead the town, to approve agendas, and for bigger, potentially hot-button issues, to put forth referendums and ballot measures.

Town managers serve their town. But they do that best by serving the Town Council. That's the job. It hasn't always been that way, though.

In chapter 2, I wrote a bit about the rise of the town manager–city council model. But I didn't really get into the history of my position. Back in the postwar suburban boom of the late 1940s and '50s, the first large generation of town managers was predominately professional engineers. They understood building and construction. They could read blueprints without asking for explanations.

However, as build-outs slowed, American society evolved with a burgeoning civil rights movement, and at the end of painful realities like redlining, some towns needed help with social engineering more than civil engineering. These towns needed trained change managers. In the 1980s and '90s, American towns moved in all kinds of directions; some communities, many in the Rust Belt, experienced brutal economic downturns, while others, particularly in the South and Southwest, grew in population and age. Cary was one of those towns that grew. Depending on the town, some town managers needed excellent interpersonal and old-school project management skills; others needed the fiscal savvy and grace to administer in the face of loss, ideally with equity and dignity.

I don't think I would have been Cary's best manager in previous decades. Although I can be demanding and detail-focused, I lack the cool steadiness of an engineer. And while I am people-focused, I wonder if I would have had the skills to navigate the turmoil of the 1960s, with all the dramatic and important social upheaval of the times. I might actually let my emotions get the best of me. I also wonder if my desire for collaboration and innovation would have had me out of step with Cary's growth spurts of the '80s and '90s, which probably required aggressive my-way-or-the-highway management. So instead, I arrived at the perfect time with the ideal—for me, at least—mandate. I like change. And I was hired here to jump-start Imagine Cary and to position the town for oncoming maturation, urbanization, and integration. The Council wanted change. Or said they wanted change.

So that's what I had to do: lead an evolution.

COUNCIL COMPOSITION

Some town councils are populated exclusively by representatives serving a specific neighborhood or area. In other councils, members are voted in by the entire town.

Cary's Town Council is a hybrid. Four of the Council members are district representatives chosen by voters within the town's four separate geographic districts, which each average around 46,000 people. The other three members are at-large representatives elected by the entire town.

In most towns, winning a seat on an at-large council requires appealing to the whole community, not just a small segment of it. And members have to constantly serve the whole community, not a special interest. That said, Cary is very lucky. By and large, the district representatives and at-large reps share the same goals. This may have to do with the town's demographic mix: the average populations of each district are similar. Or it may have to do with the approach set by Cary's previous Councils. Either way, having a Council that prefers debating and evaluating big-ticket projects is a far more enjoyable experience than working with members who only care about the issues in their own backyards.

KNOW YOUR COUNCIL

A town manager's priority is to serve their town council. But since town managers are human and somewhat ambitious, most of us will have a message and vision we'd like to impart to the council members. During

The Top of the Arc

my time in Elgin, I learned that certain members are going to be receptive to that input; they are interested in big-picture, long-term projects. There are other members, however, who will be far less collegial—both to the town manager and to their fellow council members—and far less open to big ideas. "Screw your vision," they think. "I just won an election. What does your vision do for me?"

In Elgin, I decided that as negative or uncooperative as a council member might be, I would give them my support. I would personalize my service to them, and in turn, that effort, that faith, would be returned. That meant I bent over backward at times to help them achieve their goals, even if I disagreed with them. Being supportive meant always being kind and present, even when it inconvenienced me. This policy extended beyond city business; I would take time out of my day to discuss personal issues certain council members faced and proactively try to help them. Sometimes it felt like I was a therapist or social worker.

Now, should I have done these things? Were they politically fraught? Maybe. But I wouldn't ignore people I was working with who were in dire need. That's called demonstrating empathy. Did my efforts fall outside my job description? I don't think so. My job was to manage Elgin. I needed to help the council members so that Elgin could run. Did my actions engender goodwill? Yes.

Early on, council members who required the most personal support did not embrace approving Elgin's 311 plans. But as the idea gained traction with other council members, thanks in part to our Salesforce solution, and my relationship with them grew closer, they gradually warmed to the idea. Am I recommending town managers act as unlicensed therapists? Not at all. But being flexible and service-oriented is smart. I was being empathetic. But I was also being strategic. I was keeping a potential opponent to 311 close. In this light, good people skills are good political skills.

THE ACADEMICS OF MANAGEMENT

It turns out that some of my motivations—empathy and developing strategic alliances—had other names. One of which was a well-honed phrase: "building bridges." This is the term used by one of the leading American scholars of local governance, John Nalbandian, a professor emeritus in the School of Public Affairs and Administration at the University of Kansas. In his presentations, Nalbandian has observed that "effective governance bridges the gap between political acceptability and administrative sustainability." He also noted that one of the biggest challenges of creating and reinforcing "bridge building administrative roles and problem oriented approaches" is remaining impartial, avoiding political alignment, and not becoming "administratively compromised."[1]

Bridges can be forged by many things—relationships, good ideas, expedience. But Nalbandian, who I admire for his cut-to-the-chase practicality, has said that what must be bridged are the "arenas of what is politically acceptable with what is administratively feasible." In other words, finding out what the members of the town council want and evaluating what the local government can do—technically or budget-wise—is what has to happen.

For Nalbandian, effective bridge-building methods include inviting third parties into discussions. New input creates new possibilities for the issues that need to be confronted. This creates an atmosphere of collaboration, which can reduce hierarchy and political power plays. For example, when you bring in world-class landscape architects to talk about park design, most council members are unlikely to offer laundry lists of their own ideas; they will listen to experts. Then they can share expert opinions with their constituents. All this creates a structure of planned engagement. By consulting, involving, and collaborating, a bridge—that magically stable connection—is built to empower all.

The Top of the Arc

FROM THEORY TO ACTION

In Cary, there are seven members of the Council, including the Mayor.

That means there are seven people who have ideas and opinions, who have aspirations for themselves and their community, who want to serve.

That means there are seven people who will have questions about proposals and about previous initiatives.

That means there are seven people who will want to know what the other six people in the Council are thinking about the current proposals *and* what those six people thought about previous initiatives.

That means there are seven people who may be fighting insomnia over whether to approve a bond referendum or run for office again.

And that means there are seven people who, through the course of their day, may be getting complaints from Cary citizens—about a delay in leaf collection, about a water main break, about the need for more pickleball courts, about a dearth of parking spaces, about the need for a cricket pitch or a community talent contest.

My primary job is to be there for those seven people whenever they need me and however they need me so I can help further Council goals. Those exchanges help me do what I was hired to do: be the senior change agent for Cary. Again, I'm not driving the agenda and I'm not approving it. I'm advising, informing, suggesting. I am their partner. And what do good partners do? Just ask any marriage counselor! They listen.

But a town manager doesn't just have one partner. Every council member is their partner.

Good partners also instill confidence. I don't believe in blowing smoke or staging pep rallies when faced with an impending massacre. But being realistic and positive is important. Making lemonade out of lemons happens. Helping council members by outlining a process or helping them strategize is a big part of the job. So is preparing them for obstacles, listening to their fears and frustrations, even engaging them about possible failure. I frequently find myself engaged in speculative

How to Be a Good Town Manager

equations: "In order to do X, Q has to happen first, followed by J. Then we'll be in a position to vote on doing X."

When you listen to your partners, you can also help them identify alliances; you can suggest they discuss their priority issue with a member who might share a similar view. A town manager should help partners find partners—there's no point in being possessive or exclusive with a specific council member; it's an open relationship! They all need each other as they try to navigate toward success. And in the case of Cary, it's helpful to remember that success has been defined by Imagine Cary. The Council members are just trying to find the best way to get there, and the town manager is the hybrid traffic cop, concierge, fixer, and group therapist. We lead by listening, suggesting, and organizing.

24/7.

This is the hard part. But it's also often the most gratifying part. The effective town manager needs to be present, which is different from being possessive or exclusive.

You need to be supportive, not just when an initiative wins approval, but when it doesn't. Sometimes a passion project of a council member falls on deaf ears. Sometimes a vote supports a proposal that seems misguided to a member. In these instances, you can listen and appreciate someone else's feeling of loss. You can also ask about what's been learned and what the council member would do differently next time. These discussions may lead to new plans and new outcomes. Navigating conflict is part of managing a board, and keeping unity and focus on the town's higher goals—even during times of disagreement—is, well, good governance.

As for Allison Hutchins's gracious quote that opens this chapter, yes, helping seven very passionate people serve Cary to the best of their abilities can be time-consuming. But it is gratifying work because we are all committed to creating something new, something that didn't exist previously, and hopefully, something that improves on what existed before. So I am very grateful that Cary's Council members value and strive for the best, broadest outcomes.

That is why my hardest day in Cary would be my easiest day in Elgin.

THE COUNCIL STRIKES BACK

I know what skills I rely on to help the Town Council help the town itself. Obviously, the ability to ask questions and listen closely to the responses is central to my job and is also a part of OneCary culture. With that idea in mind, my collaborator asked the Council members the following question: What are the most important skills that every town manager should have? Here's what my bosses—in alphabetical order—said:

> I think leadership is very important, providing compassion and empathy for the people who work for the leader and empowering them to make decisions and to be able to speak up. I think that is very critical because—and I always say this to Sean—if your staff is happy, they will work very, very hard for you. For me, that is number one. And then, from a town manager perspective, having the policy understanding, making sure you have that financial knowledge of how the town needs to run, and understanding the dynamics of different leadership. I can't even envy Sean because he has seven people with different mindsets that he has to manage. So having excellent communication skills, interpersonal skills, and . . . a vision but also the ability to look at the finer details are also important.
> —Sarika Bansal, first-term Town Council member

Look, you could probably ChatGPT this question and come up with the whole great list: thoughtful leadership, high emotional intelligence, financially savvy. But what does Sean bring that is different than if I were going to categorize and compare municipal town managers with each other? One of the things he does really well is, he's really adaptable. To the point where he's like Gumby. Very often, I'll throw something at him. He has a Lori list, which is my list of priorities, and I'll say,

"I want this." And he'll say, "OK, well, do you have to have it that way? What are the other ways that you could possibly have it?" He's incredibly adaptable. There have been multiple times where I've yelled at him when he really pissed me off. Right? So he can, at least for me, he can take it. He's good as both a manager and being managed, and those are both really hard things to hold on to at the same time.
—Lori Bush, four-term Town Council member

Definitely, communication is key, both listening—like *truly* listening—and also being able to relay that information. Sean is really amazing in making sure that all of our perspectives [are] seen and heard and are somehow cohesive. A town manager also should understand timing. You know, asking members, "Do you want to come to Council with all of these things or should we prioritize them?" So being adaptive is really important. I can't even imagine what it must be like to have a job that could completely change based on who's elected. I mean, how could you not be really adaptive? So I think a town manager needs to listen to all perspectives, and help us to find our voice, and be receptive and communicate.
—Michelle Craig, first-term Town Council member

There's a human element to a really great town manager where the human experience, the intangibles that don't fit into a spreadsheet well, are just as important as the dollars and cents and the ins and outs of running a very big business. So it's almost an expanded skill set with a significant human element. And if you have that special sauce, that human element, and you combine it with a really excellent business acumen, each of those two things is equally important. One or the other won't a great town manager make—it has to be both of those.
—Carissa Kohn-Johnson, first-term Town Council member

I'll tell you what I looked for when we were hiring Sean, because we talked to a lot of people. I wanted a manager who could listen to what the concerns and interests of the Council were and would respond, saying, "I understand what you want to accomplish, and let me tell you how that would be accomplished. And I will tell you the pros and cons of doing it or not doing it." That's because I wanted the Council to have the right to make the decision with all of the information. I didn't want us to be capped in our possibilities by the preferences of the manager or the staff members. And so what I saw in Sean when we were interviewing him was a person who says, "Let me tell you how it would happen. Let me tell you how we can get to solving that." And then he gave us the options. He gives us options all the time so that we can make an informed decision. And I think that is a nuance in great management.

—Jennifer Bryson Robinson, six-term Town Council member

If you go back to Stephen Covey and his book *The Seven Habits of Highly Effective People,* one of the things that I remember from when I was in middle management and trying to improve myself is this whole idea of being able to see the end. Sean is great at always having a vision for the end. You have that, and then you work backward on how to get there. Sometimes I get faux-mad—I'm not really mad, of course—because Sean has a way of knowing what the end is and working you there and *you* don't know it yet. So to me, that's a critical part of leadership: understanding where you want to go and being able to figure out how to get there.

—Jack Smith, nine-term Town Council member

The first thing is they have to totally understand the vision of the Council, which is hard if you have a Council going in seven different directions. I think he's got to have good relationships with all the Council members so he can have good conversations with them. And I think he's got to balance all those personalities. And right there is a miracle if you could do that. He's got to totally understand the staff and their strengths and be a visionary on top of that.

—Harold Weinbrecht, Cary Mayor and six-term Town Council member

PURPOSE AND IMPERFECTION

I was in a meeting where a debate came up about the purpose of government. And I repeated what I mentioned back in chapter 3, that I thought the government exists to ensure the safety of the community. But safety isn't just about fires and crime. Government needs to provide space for new ideas, for disagreement, and yes, for failure. All these "dangerous" elements of humanity need to be able to flourish without fear.

So a town manager needs to operate from a starting point of empathy, whether they're dealing with the council or a departmental issue. New initiatives, from establishing new office procedures to introducing new technology, can be difficult to master. Meanwhile, people have lives that exist outside of government. A member of the staff may have substance abuse issues, or financial burdens, or a health crisis. A member of their family may be suffering. These things can impact performance and cause problems at work. But if a town manager approaches these challenges with empathy throughout the organization, as opposed to instantly writing someone off, then there are wins all around. You've established a culture that seeks to uplift instead of punish and that aspires to evolve toward the most positive outcome possible. Sometimes a team member isn't in the right position. Sometimes a personality may not jibe with our culture. Sometimes, they need a career change. Our organization works to find these alternatives.

Leadership advisor Montana Rozmus made a few comments about my town manager style to a friend who described it as one of the nicest left-handed compliments he'd ever heard. Then he insisted I share it because, apparently, sharing—or oversharing—is what I do: "I would

The Top of the Arc

say Sean just has a very comfortable relationship with vulnerability that is not usual or normal in senior leaders. He's cried in group dialogues that I've been in. And it's interesting, because he will kind of have that quick moment of maybe a little touch of embarrassment, but then the people around the room, you can tell that they love him so much, because he's willing to go there. And because he allows himself to be imperfect so they can be imperfect too."

CHAPTER 10
THE TOP OF THE ARC AND THE IMPORTANCE OF REINVENTION

I want us to excel in all things. The small things, the big things... everything!

—Sarika Bansal, first-term Cary Town Council member

Like many devoted public sector members, I suffer from occasional pangs of cynicism about the motives driving the private sector. That said, I admire the vision and innovative mojo of tech giants, engineering firms, medical researchers, and the endless legion of start-up entrepreneurs in America. Thanks to inventors and investors, the world is a truly amazing place.

But given the frequent media hype and lionization of private sector big guys and wannabes, it's easy to forget that the government has been a source of phenomenal innovation. So much of what shapes our lives in the US has been the direct and indirect result of government decisions. Consider, for a moment, the impact of the 1956 National Interstate and Defense Highways Act, which President Eisenhower initially

The Top of the Arc

floated in his 1954 State of the Union speech. It led to incalculable change—41,000 miles of highway had a domino effect on America's development. I'm not sure Cary would have grown as it did without its proximity to highways. The new infrastructure not only helped create a trucking industry that employed between 5 to 10 percent of the workforce but also freed manufacturers from rail line dependence. It also allowed new factories and towns to be developed and built anywhere. Travel opened up and sped up, creating a new multibillion-dollar domestic tourist industry, which, in turn, fuels other adjacent sectors, such as advertising, retail, and food and beverage.

Challenged and inspired by John F. Kennedy, the federal government, in the form of the National Aeronautics and Space Administration (NASA), put a man on the moon. The research involved in that project resulted in the invention of new materials and technologies that surround us today—from sportswear to UV-blocking sunglasses to cordless devices and so much more. Meanwhile, the federally funded Defense Advanced Research Projects Agency invented the internet, the backbone of the tech revolution that is still exploding.[1]

Decades later, 1,500 miles from Silicon Valley, Cary was able to innovate using that very invention when we opted for the cloud-powered Salesforce platform for our 311 service. That, as I've documented, led to the town staff investing themselves in the rollout. The boat was rocked. We were creating, or reinventing, our roles and processes. Unstated in all this at the time was that we were striving to stay at the top of the arc.

And speaking of creating new roles, I want to mention another mold worth breaking: the negative perception of local government workers. You've probably heard the clichéd comments about public sector employees:

"Government workers are just there to get their pensions."

"Government workers lack motivation."

"Nobody gets rewarded for new ideas in government, so there's no advantage to rocking the boat."

The Top of the Arc and the Importance of Reinvention

Statements like this make me furious for many reasons but mostly because, in my experience, they are simply not true. Most public sector employees want to execute their jobs well. They take pride in excellence. The launch of Cary 311 was a confirmation of this. Staff developed new skills, got new titles, and worked with new equipment. While these areas of personal growth might translate into monetizable skills in the future, in the short term, they paid off with increases in confidence and pride and a sense of empowerment.

But even if there's a fraction of truth in those negative government worker stereotypes, guess what? They don't solely pertain to government employees. Not even close. A former Fortune 500 company vice president told me those comments could have applied to some staff members. "But there's one difference," they said. "Nobody at the company was just working for a pension—*because the company didn't offer any*!"

Cary, by breaking out of our molds and embracing ambiguity-tinged plans, encouraged intentional momentum, not stagnation. As the culture around decision-making changed, the town bureaucracy mutated, new organizational paradigms surfaced, and yes, people were rewarded for new ideas and increased effort.

Cary evolved.

We must keep evolving.

We are creating a local government that doesn't exist because we are building a town that doesn't exist either.

Oh, sure. Cary exists. Absolutely. It's on maps. We live here. A friend just wrote to me to say he saw four schools in town appear on a list of North Carolina's top 20 public schools.

The Cary of *tomorrow*, however, does not exist yet in concrete terms. That is what we are creating. We are following the Imagine Cary Community Plan. We continued working on its next installment, writing the story to help us remain who we are—a community that engages in focused, calculated evolution to create a better environment for us all. In fall 2024, the town published updates to the plan: a new preface; the inclusion of the 2021 Cary Housing Plan into the document's LIVE chapter, complete with updated data; a new chapter called ENRICH, which documents the environmental challenges and opportunities; and, finally, an upgrade to our SERVE chapter, zooming in on all the vital infrastructure sectors we must address, including road maintenance, transit, water, wastewater, solid waste, and public safety.[2]

You know: Staying at the top of the arc. By the people, for the people.

There is an argument—and my associate Dan Ault is a strong proponent of it—that a local government is better positioned to be a change agent than a national government.

"It doesn't matter if you're a dictatorship, a monarchy, or democracy; we're all facing the same challenges," Dan asserted. "If you look around the world, no form of government is really more stable than the other. Strangely, the stability is on the ground locally. We're all dealing with the same issues, so you can actually have a common infrastructure that can work together globally. In other words, when I look at this mosaic, I'm making value choices for my community. But I also am able to understand that this is having a global impact. And I look at a different mosaic, that's not mine. But maybe something from mine can help, or vice versa."

While I will politely disagree with Dan's riff about central governments—a totalitarian dictatorship can enforce widespread change, for better or for worse, a great deal more quickly than a democracy—I do agree with his points about the flexibility and stability of local government. And one of the things that bolsters our ability to evolve is rooted in political will. Within a democracy, it is usually easier to unite a small population than it is to unite a large population. Larger communities are more susceptible to fragmentation; more people often translates into increased special interest groups, outside influences, and other forces. There is also the potential for disunity that comes with communities with many districts. When leaders care only about what goes on in their backyard, it can be destabilizing. In these instances, the political will, the unity, and the support required to evolve can dissipate.

The Top of the Arc and the Importance of Reinvention

Building political will is trickier than ever. It used to be that all citizens were potential stakeholders, but grabbing that stake and making noise about it was not very easy. Now you don't have to wait for a town meeting to be heard. The ability to amplify views on social media platforms gives stakeholders a new, powerful, easy-access loudspeaker. Citizens can advocate, pontificate, agitate, and bloviate on all sorts of issues on X, Reddit, Instagram, and dozens of other platforms—all to stoke passions before town hall meetings.

"There's pressure to treat everybody's opinions equally," Montana Rozmus, the leadership expert I've worked with, says. "But is the ordinary citizen the same as somebody who has a PhD in this exact subject you're dealing with versus the bureaucrat who understands the logistics of actually doing something? I think there's this balance between wanting to be inclusive and taking feedback from your constituents, from the town, from all stakeholders, and saying, 'Hey, wait a minute, we've been doing this for 30 years. We know that the safe way doesn't necessarily work that well. We want to try something that might be a little bit less safe. But it requires that people trust us just long enough to start to see some effects.'"

That trust is another example of political will. And Montana notes that building it requires vigilance and focus: "Any kind of organization has its cultural level of risk tolerance, and governments are kind of on the low end of that scale just because of the diversity of constituents and the level of visibility required to the public. It's almost similar to a public company versus a private one. In a private company, you could spend $30,000 on office furniture and no one would even know it, whereas in a public company, there's some level of public expectation of disclosure. Then, in the government, the scrutiny is much more intense because there are records that you can go online and look at, and people can see you at Trader Joe's and tell you how stupid they thought that decision was. So I would say those are all the pressures on an organization not to do anything differently, even if everybody sort of agrees that something needs to be done."

The Top of the Arc

In other words, not evolving, keeping your head down, and staying the course are the easier leadership options. But what kind of leadership is that?

Harnessing the power of local government is more than just pragmatic and inspirational. It's essential for our well-being and for future generations.

It is very easy and convenient to think of hot-button issues such as energy use, climate change, or supply chain issues as purely global concerns rather than local ones. I get it. Cary has had no carbon-spewing factories in the past. Even though we traded farmland for human habitation, we didn't outsource our local crops to China. Still, it does seem logical that local communities *everywhere* have been warming the climate since humans discovered fire and started cutting down forests. Every local community has been contributing simultaneously.

Now the same thing needs to happen today in reverse. We need to cool the climate locally. If local governments were to spearhead a ton of micro actions, those small initiatives would grow into macro actions. Does that smack of idealism? Only if you are a cynic or in denial. It is, I submit, a question of logic, of the math we learn in elementary school. Incremental changes can add up to big changes. We can do it. It just requires localized innovation, developing energy-efficient communities, sharing information and best practices, and yes, sacrifice. These are actions that can and must be done to sustain the governments, the communities, the world we want to live in.

Cary is taking these actions, by the way. The Imagine Cary Community Plan lists the town's land use and growth policies. Here are the first four bullet points regarding policy goals for new initiatives:

- Provide daily shopping and services needs (such as grocery stores, banking, dry cleaning, etc.) within about ½ to 1 mile of most households. This provides more options to access daily shopping, dining, and services needs via walking, biking, or driving, due to the close proximity to home;

The Top of the Arc and the Importance of Reinvention

- Reduce traffic on major streets by reducing the average length of vehicular trips for shopping and services, and by providing opportunities to make such trips from the neighborhood via local road connections;
- Reduce thoroughfare traffic and minimize the number of required lanes on thoroughfares by avoiding continuous strip development;
- Improve air quality and energy consumption by enabling shorter trips for shopping and services.[3]

These are not earth-shattering, radical policies. And that's the point. They are incremental. One change at a time, we will reshape our environment. Just by increasing population density, we will, ideally, create economies of scale and reduce energy and water usage. Our existing initiatives to promote sustainability and environmental resilience will become more efficient as the town grows vertically. Cary was the first town in North Carolina to provide free, year-round curbside collection and recycling for residents with used fats, oils, and grease, which are reconstituted to help generate the biodiesel that fuels our town trucks. The town also picks up computer and electronic appliances for recycling along with biweekly collections of other recyclable materials. Developments such as Fenton will allow for more energy-efficient collection by consolidating collection points.

There are many other sustainability projects flourishing in Cary, including the creation of a 1.89-megawatt solar energy farm on town-owned land. But among the most ambitious were driven by Cary's Environmental Advisory Board, which provided a strategy to reduce carbon emissions, address climate change, and create climate resiliency. The Council accepted the recommendations to reduce carbon emissions by 25 percent by 2025 and 100 percent by 2040.

It's not idealism if you commit to a culture dedicated to envisioning and igniting evolution. It's reality.

FEEDING THE DREAM, BOLSTERING THE ARC

I want to return, briefly, to the issue of local taxes. Or, as I like to sometimes think of it, legally mandated, community-focused diversified investment. As I noted earlier, a 2024 referendum vote and follow-up survey told the Cary Town Council that a majority of voters did not want property tax increases at that time to pay for $590 million of community improvements.

You might think this was a no-brainer. Who in their right mind wants to pay higher taxes? But the fact is, 45 percent of voters were fine with doing just that. I was reassured by and grateful for that statistic. This book is about a lot of things—good governance, innovation, cocreation—but it's also about defining and investing in our vision of ourselves. And that means it is about growth.

I want to propose a twist on Benjamin Franklin's famous saying, "In this world, nothing is certain except death and taxes."[4] I'm not about to argue with the brilliant Mr. Franklin. But I do want to suggest another certainty: growth for local government is unsustainable without taxes. They are a fact of life. And life, by the way, is the opposite of Mr. Franklin's inarguable certainty: death.

Staying at the top of the arc for a business, institution, or government requires ambition, risk, intense focus, and investment and *reinvestment*. Capital reinvestment is needed to stay at the top of the arc, and the easiest, most equitable device for obtaining that capital that I know of remains taxation.

STAYING AT THE TOP OF THE ARC

When I think about my mission to help Cary create a government that doesn't exist and our constantly evolving culture, sometimes I glimpse different meanings within my ambiguous phrase. If a town or

The Top of the Arc and the Importance of Reinvention

government constantly evolves, it never has a fixed state of being. It exists—but not in a finite sense.

With this in mind, I want to return to the title of this book and the words I quoted from the plaque in Downtown Cary Park: "Arcs serve as a personal reminder . . . that it is up to each of us to keep Cary 'at the top of the arc.' Parks, people, even entire communities evolve, and we—all of us—shoulder the incredible responsibility for creating and recreating the best Cary possible."

It is very difficult to stay at the top of the arc—in business, in politics, or as I mentioned earlier, while surfing. Landscapes are constantly shifting. The wave you're riding crests and collapses. External forces cannot be predicted or controlled. Things change. In 2002, the top 10 most valuable American companies included General Electric, Microsoft, ExxonMobil, Walmart, Pfizer, Citigroup, Intel, Johnson & Johnson, AIG, and IBM. Twenty years later, only Microsoft remained on that list, second to Apple, followed by the likes of Alphabet/Google, Amazon, Tesla, Berkshire Hathaway, Nvidia, Meta/Facebook, Visa, and United Health.[5]

It may be sobering to realize that companies that are staffed with, supposedly, the best and the brightest (not to mention seemingly bottomless coffers of cash) can't stay on the top of the arc. But let's learn from that. This is why reinvention is critical to creating a local government that doesn't exist. Without reinvention, you get stasis. Momentum stops. You fall. Some nearby town lures a new megabusiness that you hoped to entice. A neighboring community raises money for a theater complex similar to the one you wanted to develop.

How do you ensure the momentum for reinvention? This is a question I've been grappling with and trying to demonstrate throughout this book. Frequently, I'd find myself wondering, What is it about Cary that can be replicated in other local governments?

Part of the answer, at least with regard to never hitting a plateau, is that towns must dare to dream. Of course, civic duty requires that I amend this old saw. Towns must dare to dream responsibly. Responsible dreaming might seem like a contradiction in terms. But good

The Top of the Arc

local governance—starting with an involved citizenry and a wise town council—should instinctively put up some guardrails. The law tells you what you can and can't do.

In the end, the answers I keep coming back to involve the investments a town can make. The blueprint for creating an effective local government that doesn't exist—but stays at the top of the arc—hinges on these broad concepts:

1. Invest in people—they are the who, the why, the what, and the how of government.
2. Have a town council that not only aspires to create a great present and an even more amazing future but is mandated to do so.
3. To ensure the previous point, voters should demand the cocreation of an ambitious, adaptive, actionable plan for the future.
4. Create an adaptive culture, empowering leadership at all levels so that everyone in the local government feels invested and engaged in their job.
5. Codify that culture of support to inspire creativity and positivity, not fear, and value desired outcomes and analysis ahead of politics.
6. With #1–5 in place, now invest in projects.
7. Be comfortable with uncertainty on the journey to discovering the best outcome.
8. Collaborate with both coworkers and outside experts.
9. Cocreate more ambitious, adaptive, and actionable plans.

These are the things that drive our cities and towns forward. I listed them as a sequence, but I suspect they can grow in parallel because, as the Cary story demonstrates, evolution takes time (and can make a mess). New cultures must be nurtured and grown. It doesn't happen overnight, and it takes a shared vision. It takes a community that

The Top of the Arc and the Importance of Reinvention

cares about people and understands that change—evolution—isn't the enemy; it is the inevitable future. Evolution also never ends.

We must acknowledge that by defining and creating our local government, we can shape that change, that future, into something we desire.

Together.

ACKNOWLEDGMENTS

I spent what feels like countless hours attempting to name all the people who have helped me and molded my perspectives on leadership, culture, and city administration. After a conversation with Ron Heifetz, I eventually realized that no matter how hard I tried, I'd never be able to name them all. I do take solace in knowing that I have, over the years, expressed my gratitude to them directly.

Even so, there are a few I must call out.

First and foremost, I am grateful to my family for their love and tolerance as I spend the vast majority of my life at work. Their compassion and constant support help me get through the high highs and low lows that come with public service.

My success as Cary's manager—and ours as a community—is directly tied to the welcome and support I received and continue to enjoy each day from Cary's residents, businesspeople, community leaders, and phenomenal town staff. Each and all consistently put Cary first, and that's what keeps us at the top of the arc.

I also must recognize the members of the Cary Town Council, 2016 to today, all of whom made the book possible. As individuals and collectively as a team, each person and each Council has embraced and challenged me, making me better at what I do and who I am. Most importantly, they have let me into their lives, and I'm so much richer for this gift.

To the actual words on the page and the publishing of this book, I call out the efforts of Seth Kaufman, Susan Moran, Allison Hutchins, Kristy Buchanan, Kerry Harville, Sarah Acker, Hal Goodtree, and Diana Hong.

Acknowledgments

Without their experience, expertise, professionalism, collaboration, and attention to detail, our story would not have been told.

Cary was established in 1871, and more than 150 years later, I am delighted to have been chosen to walk after and alongside others whose tales have intersected with mine, sharing their joys, losses, and successes. Their vision, resilience, humor, vulnerability, and humanity have left an everlasting imprint on this book, giving it depth and authenticity and ensuring that it's just the *next* chapter of Cary's story—not the last.

And finally, to the readers who contribute their own experiences and interpretations to these pages, I am humbled by your presence. Your engagement with these words, your openness to listen and reflect as you work to develop and build community in whatever way you define it, will make governments around the globe better.

With appreciation,
Sean

NOTES

PREFACE

1 Except for the town clerk and the town attorney, who are also hired by the Town Council.

CHAPTER 1

1 "Summit on the Future Beckons Citizens to Imagine Cary," Cary Public Information Office, August 15, 2013, https://www.carync.gov/Home/Components/News/News/9987/.

2 "QuickFacts: Cary Town, North Carolina," US Census Bureau, accessed December 3, 2024, https://www.census.gov/quickfacts/fact/table/carytownnorthcarolina/POP060210.

3 Troy L. Kickler, "Research Triangle Park," North Carolina History Project, accessed November 25, 2024, https://northcarolinahistory.org/encyclopedia/research-triangle-park.

4 Elliott Davis Jr., "These States Are Bringing in More Residents Than They're Losing," *U.S. News & World Report*, December 5, 2023, https://www.usnews.com/news/best-states/articles/these-states-are-bringing-in-more-residents-than-theyre-losing.

5 Town of Cary, *The Cary 2040 Community Plan: A Comprehensive Plan for the Town of Cary*, January 24, 2017, https://www.carync.gov/home/showpublisheddocument/14045/637620214610270000.

Notes

6 "Cary Population to Explode," DowntownCary, accessed December 5, 2024, https://web.archive.org/web/20221101005949/https://downtowncary.org/cary-population-set-to-explode-citizens-yawn/.

CHAPTER 2

1 Michael McGrath, "The First One Hundred Years: A Brief History of the National Civic Review," *National Civic Review*, March 22, 2011, https://www.thefreelibrary.com/The+first+one+hundred+years:+a+brief+history+of+the+National+Civic...-a0255242418.

2 Originally founded as the National Municipal League. See the history page of the National Civic League: https://www.nationalcivicleague.org/history/.

3 "Staunton, Virginia: Birthplace of City Manager Form of Government," Staunton City Hall, accessed December 5, 2024, https://web.archive.org/web/20051120051230/http://www.staunton.va.us/default.asp?pageID=B94197C5-F4F9-427D-938A-4CFCCF4929DF.

4 "Model City Charter—9th Edition: Introduction," National Civic League, accessed December 5, 2024, https://www.nationalcivicleague.org/model-city-charter-9th-edition-introduction/.

CHAPTER 3

1 "Baltimore's 311 Non-emergency Number," C-SPAN, July 14, 1997, https://www.c-span.org/video/?87969-1/baltimores-311-emergency-number#.

2 Dan and I also had one strange thing in common. We both recall wanting to be city managers at ridiculously young ages. I remember

being in the car with my parents when my mother spotted our mayor's car swerving. This was during the rise of Mothers Against Drunk Drivers in the early 1980s, and I was very upset to hear the mayor would do something so horrible. My father told me not to worry: "The town manager is really the one who runs things." Suddenly, I wasn't thinking about our mayor crashing; I was thinking about this job where someone was more powerful than a mayor. It was like a real-life Wizard of Oz who really did have special powers. As for Dan, he remembers becoming hooked when his hometown in Wisconsin hired its first village manager, and his parents explained, "He's the person that kind of runs things." Except for a flirtation with baseball, he never wanted to do anything else but work in local government.

3 Anne Moxie and Rebecca Wettemann, "ROI Case Study Salesforce City of Elgin," Nucleus Research, March 2015, https://a.sfdcstatic.com/content/dam/www/ocms/assets/pdf/misc/Salesforce_ROI_case_study_City_of_Elgin.pdf.

CHAPTER 4

1 Why are growth and evolution so important? That is a complicated question. But a short answer might be "Because communities need a continual source of revenue to sustain themselves." An even shorter answer might be "Look at the decline of Rust Belt communities." When America began outsourcing and offshoring our manufacturing businesses, those towns experienced steep declines.

2 Fact: There are always unintended consequences.

3 Ronald A. Heifetz and Marty Linsky, *Leadership on the Line: Staying Alive through the Dangers of Leading* (Cambridge, MA: Harvard Business Review Press, 2002), 26.

Notes

CHAPTER 5

1 "OneCary Culture," Cary, accessed December 5, 2024, https://www.carync.gov/connect-engage/jobs-employees/onecary-culture.

CHAPTER 6

1 "Public Trust in Government: 1958–2023," Pew Center for Research, September 19, 2023, https://www.pewresearch.org/politics/2023/09/19/public-trust-in-government-1958-2023/.

2 Jeffrey M. Jones, "Americans Trust Local Government Most, Congress Least," Gallup Politics, October 13, 2023, https://news.gallup.com/poll/512651/americans-trust-local-government-congress-least.aspx.

3 "Total Employed Persons in the United States in 2023, by Industry," Statista Research Department, July 5, 2024, https://www.statista.com/statistics/200143/employment-in-selected-us-industries/.

CHAPTER 7

1 Daniel Jonas Roche, "The Great Lawn: Downtown Cary Park in North Carolina by OJB and Machado Silvetti Creates a New Square in the Research Triangle," *Architect's Newspaper*, December 7, 2023, https://www.archpaper.com/2023/12/cary-park-north-carolina-ojb-machado-silvetti-new-square/.

CHAPTER 8

1 Town of Cary, *The Cary 2040 Community Plan: A Comprehensive Plan for the Town of Cary*, January 24, 2017, 106, https://www.carync.gov/home/showpublisheddocument/14242/637620234121130000.

2 Peggy Van Scoyoc, "Cary History: The Early Days of South Hills Mall," *CaryCitizen*, November 5, 2021, https://carycitizen.news/2021/11/05/cary-history-the-early-days-of-south-hills-mall/.

3 Kristen Johnson, "'Consider the Most Vulnerable': Cary Budget Proposes Tax Increase for Owners," *News & Observer*, May 28, 2024, https://www.newsobserver.com/news/local/counties/wake-county/article288584459.html.

4 "11/05/2024 Official General Election Results—Wake," North Carolina State Board of Elections, accessed December 27, 2024, https://er.ncsbe.gov/?election_dt=11/05/2024&county_id=92&office=REF&contest=0.

CHAPTER 9

1 John Nalbandian, "Contemporary Trends and Leadership Challenges in Local Government," ICMA, accessed December 5, 2024, https://icma.org/sites/default/files/John%20Nalbandian%20ContemporaryTrends%20and%20Leadership%20Challenges%20in%20Local%20Government%202014-06-03%20DAO%20meeting.pdf.

Notes

CHAPTER 10

1 Lest anyone think I am unaware of or unconcerned about the ecological challenges these innovations have accelerated, I am. In the subsequent pages, I discuss undoing the damage.

2 "Imagine Cary Community Plan—2024 Update," accessed January 11, 2024, https://www.carync.gov/projects-initiatives/cary-community-plan/imagine-cary-community-plan-interim-update.

3 Town of Cary, *The Cary 2040 Community Plan: A Comprehensive Plan for the Town of Cary*, January 24, 2017, 86, https://www.carync.gov/home/showpublisheddocument/14242/637620234121130000.

4 NCC staff, "Benjamin Franklin's Last Great Quote and the Constitution," National Constitution Center, November 13, 2023, https://constitutioncenter.org/blog/benjamin-franklins-last-great-quote-and-the-constitution.

5 Gary Hoover, "Most Valuable U.S. Companies 1995 through 2022," American Business History Center, July 8, 2022, accessed December 27, 2024, https://americanbusinesshistory.org/most-valuable-u-s-companies-1995-through-2022/.